ASK, GET, PERFORM

The Auditors Essential Guide to
Asking Better Questions, Getting Better Answers,
and Performing Better Audits

Robert Berry

Copyright © 2021 Robert Berry

No part of this publication may be copied, reproduced in any format, by any means, electronic or otherwise, without prior consent from the copyright owner.

This book is designed to provide information and motivation to its readers. The content is the sole expression and opinion of its author. No warranties or guarantees are expressed or implied. The author shall not be liable for psychological, emotional, financial, or commercial damages. It is the reader's responsibility to test and research any idea or practice before implementing it in his or her business activities.

First Edition, 2021
ISBN 9798591025755

Dedication

I would like to dedicate this book to the risk, audit and compliance professionals who work diligently to provide awesome services to your organization's stakeholders.

INTRODUCTION 1

THE COMMUNICATION CONUNDRUM 3

You're a Terrible Communicator 7
3 Concerns with Questions 11
Why is communication difficult? 14
5 Elements For Quality Questions 20

WHY ASK WHY? 31

The Power of Question 32
Break through Question Barriers 47

REDUCING THE COMMUNICATION CONFUSION 59

Back to Communication Basics 60
Moving Beyond the Basics 70
5 Communication Styles 71
3 Learning Styles 91

5 STEP APPROACH TO QUALITY QUESTIONS 97

Step 1 - Collaboration is Key 100
Understand your auditor personality 101
Understand Audit Client Personalities 115
Step 2 Don't Get Taken Out of Context 129
Step 3 - Check the Technique 133
4 Types of questions for Your toolkit 136
5 Critical Elements for Quality Questions 147

Let's Talk Technique *153*
7 Questions for Successful Audit Issues *159*
STEP 4 - MAKE A COMMITMENT TO CLARITY 163
5 Questions That Promote Paraphrasing *164*
STEP 5 - THE COMMUNICATION CONTINUUM 167

CONCLUSION **170**

Introduction

Curiosity is the cornerstone of internal auditing. It requires that we interact with and extract information from audit clients. This means you have to ask your clients a lot of questions. Sometimes you annoy clients with not only the questions that you ask but also how you ask.

Some auditors badger clients with bad questions and then become upset when they do not receive access to the people, information or documents requested.

But before you blame your clients, take some responsibility for how you communicate with others. After all, communication is a two-way street and breakdowns cannot always be clients' fault.

Asking questions is one of the most important parts of your job. If you cannot ask effective questions, you will not have a job long. I want you to have a long, healthy and rewarding career. That is why I wrote this book and developed the Ask, Get, Perform training course.

This book is designed to improve the quality of your questions.

Chapter 1 discusses the communication conundrum. There is one huge problem with communication. The sooner you recognize this problem, the sooner you can take measures to improve.

This chapter also addresses the 3 Concerns with Questions and 5 Critical Elements for Quality Questions.

Chapter 2 is all about the benefits of asking good questions and how to break through barriers that keep you stuck asking bad questions. By the end of this chapter, you should have more confidence and be able to quiet your negative inner thoughts.

Chapter 3 takes us back to the basics of human communication. It sets a baseline for the rest of the text. It introduces 5 communications styles. In these styles, you will recognize many of the people in your life. This chapter also shows warning signs of destructive people and offers solutions when interacting with them. This chapter is packed with information that will allow you to give clients information in ways that best fit their communication style.

Chapter 4 is the heart of asking better questions, getting better answers and performing better audits. It details a five-step approach to improving the quality of your questions with clients and colleagues. This is the bulk of the book. And that's intentional. By the end of this chapter, you will be able to identify various collaboration techniques, effectively utilize the right type of questions in each audit stage, provide clients with the appropriate amount of clarity and develop a continuous communication strategy.

Chapter One

The Communication Conundrum

> Never say mean words out of anger. Your anger will pass. But your mean words leave a scar. Use kinds words or be silent.
>
> ~ Anonymous

It was an uneventful Monday morning, that is, until the Senior Vice President of Operations popped in our office. While reviewing his risk dashboards, he noticed some strange activity and wanted us to take a look. He believed one of his store managers was padding the inventory.

The company used a third-party provider to perform the independent inventory count. While on site, we noticed that store employees prevented the third party from counting certain items. Instead, they gave the lead counter a paper with the count for items stored in a backroom. This didn't seem right. We had to take a look.

From a distance, it appeared to be a small group of items. As we moved closer, we saw three rows of pallets stacked three levels high in shrink-wrap cluttering the backroom.

We were told these were slow moving items that would be placed on the sales floor soon. The store manager did not want to break the shrink wrap to count the inventory because he did not want to create a junky backroom. This was a pitiful excuse for not allowing the inventory counters to do their job.

Breaking the shrink-wrap, we found a pile of junk filled with obsolete inventory. Some items were more than 10 years old.

As the mystery began to unravel, we discovered that it started small many years ago. The store manager took a gamble on a product he thought would make money. It failed to sell. Instead of writing the items off, he placed them in shrink wrap in the back of the store. This continued for several years until the small pile grew into a massive mound of unusable inventory.

At this point, the total damage was half a million dollars. Store personnel informed us that there may be additional inventory off-site. We called local storage facilities and discovered that the store manager was using three storage facilities for so called 'slow moving' products. In all, he was concealing more than a million dollars in obsolete items.

The store manager's scheme to conceal his crime was not complicated. Over the years, he would move items in the middle of the night from the store to the storage facilities. In the beginning, the amounts were immaterial. He developed a good relationship with the third party provider who did not notice that the dollar amounts had grown from minimal to millions.

During the engagement, we made a point to provide the Senior Vice President weekly updates. In the end, we compiled a report describing the fraud and the dollar impact. When we presented the report to management, the Senior Vice President became upset with us.

We did not understand his behavior. After all, he requested our services. We investigated and reported what we found. Yet we were seen as the bad guys for performing good work.

Turns out, the Senior Vice President and the store manager were close friends. And while he did indeed ask for the review, The Senior Vice President hoped it would clear his friend's name.

Unfortunately, the facts did not trump his feelings. The status updates did nothing to change his bias. The final report was ineffective.

We thought we had done everything right. Unfortunately, the things we were taught about audit client communications failed.

Therein lies the communication conundrum. We are all terrible communicators.

In this situation, it seemed like we did everything right. We were objective and independent. We gathered facts and communicated with our client regularly. What happened?

It can be easy to blame the client for the debacle. Afterall, he should have been able to handle the truth. But communication is an evolving process dependent on several rational and irrational factors. It is a give and take. A two-way street. It is any other catchy analogy you want to add to say that it is complicated.

Our biggest failure in this project was that we failed to recognize our client's bias. We believed that following a scripted methodology would provide a good outcome. But we saw signs of his bias early on. We chose to ignore them. While there is plenty of blame to pass around in this incident, the fact is we are all terrible communicators.

If you don't believe me, check out the next section.

You're a Terrible Communicator

What is the most important relationship in your life? Go ahead. Think about it for a moment. For most of us, the most important person is a spouse or a partner, boyfriend or girlfriend, friends or family.

For couples, you find that special person and stand before your friends and family to profess your love for them. You vow to be together forever. That marriage or union signifies an important relationship.

But if we are such great communicators, why is it that first marriages in the United States end in divorce over 60% of the time? And according to most sources, one of the top 5 reasons cited for divorce is poor communication.

So let me just get this straight. This is an important relationship and over 60% of the time, we get it wrong. And when we get it wrong, it's always the other person's fault. Right?

And because it's always the other person's fault, we do it again. The second time around has to be better right? We vow to be a better people picker. Well, in the United States, more than 70% of second marriages end in divorce.

But like baseball, the third time's the charm. Surely you will not strike out. The third time you will make it work. Unfortunately, more than 80% of third marriages in the United States end in divorce.

Who are we fooling? This tells us that we are all terrible at communicating. And it seems as though the more we practice, the worse we become.

Seriously, We Are All Terrible Communicators

But if you're still not a believer, let me tell you about my friend Jill.

She's smart, sassy and single. She knows what she wants in life and is not afraid to go after it. Occasionally she talks to me about the dating scene. She wants someone who is tall, intelligent, has hair and is funny. She's not an overly complicated person. Not in a rush to get in a relationship, but not running from one either. Unfortunately, she has strange encounters on the dating scene. The most recent, at Starbucks.

Most mornings you can find her drinking her favorite latte at her favorite location. One day while enjoying some 'me time' before work, an attractive guy walks in. He must have felt her staring because they lock eyes like high school sweethearts who found one another after 20 years apart.

He ordered a latte and looked at Jill, "I don't know you, but I'd like to sit down and talk to you for a few minutes. And if we like each other, maybe we can move forward with something special."

Admiring his stunning physique, Jill said, "Sure."

They found the perfect quiet spot and talked.

After hours of conversation, Jill's new friend needed to leave. But before he departed, he looked at her and said, "It was a pleasure meeting you. Now I have one thing to ask before I go"

At this point, Jill was pretty excited. "He's going to ask for my number", she thought.

He takes her by the hand, drops to one knee and says "Jill, I've only known you for a short time".

She laughs hysterically because she thinks this is another one of his jokes.

"Let's just get married," he continues.

She laughs.

"Jill. I'm not joking. I know what I want. And what I want is you".

There she stood, phone in hand, expecting him to ask for her number. Jill's excitement turned to disgust. She thought he was a nice person. And now he's blowing it.

What happened in this situation? What made her turn from excited to upset? Was his question inappropriate? Or was she just crazy for not wanting to take the bull by the horns and seize the day? We'll catch up with Jill later and see what went wrong here. For now, let's turn our attention to the three concerns with questions.

3 Concerns with Questions

Three things we should consider when it comes to questions.

First, asking questions is the hardest thing you will ever do.
Asking questions is a lifelong commitment. Think about it. As children, you ask your parents' permission to (1) go outside to play, (2) stay up past curfew, (3) go to that cool new summer camp and much more.

As an adult, you ask employers to (1) hire you by way of a job application, (2) pay you a fair wage, and (3) allow you to take time off for vacation. You ask friends and family for favors. You ask strangers for assistance. Questions cannot be avoided. Often it is difficult to know who to ask, what to ask and how to ask.

Second, there is power in asking questions.
If you ask the right questions the right way, you can harness the power in questioning.

If you have ever been pulled over by the police, you'll notice the first thing they ask is "Do you know why I stopped you?" If you are smart, you will say no.

But let's imagine you respond, "Yes. I was speeding. I was doing 65mph in a 55mph zone."

What if he pulled you over because your vehicle had a broken tail light? Because he asked a question that you openly answered, he can now write you a ticket for two infractions, speeding and a broken tail light.

This example speaks to the power of asking. Asking the right question, to the right person, and at the right time can drastically change any situation.

Third, there is more to asking questions than asking questions.
As auditors, we should know this better than anyone. Take the retail inventory incident from earlier. We answered the critical question about the inventory. The amounts were wrong because someone was committing fraud. However, the response to the investigation was not what we expected. We provided adequate answers and yet somehow were still labeled as the bad guys.

What does this mean for auditors?

First, we must acknowledge that asking questions is difficult.
I can be the first to admit that I am sometimes nervous around new clients, industries or processes. I worked for several years as a business process consultant for one of the Big 4 accounting and

consulting firms. I was constantly moving from client to client and industry to industry. Getting accustomed to a new environment, culture or people required me to ask a lot of questions.

Often it is hard to admit you don't know something. It's even harder to admit you need help. But that is exactly what you should do. If you're facing a process you are unfamiliar with, ask a question. If you have been assigned a new client, ask a question.

Unfortunately, having the ability to ask a question does not mean you will be effective. Thankfully you're in the right place to talk about effective questioning techniques.

Second, be aware of the power of questions.
One audit report has the power to change an individual, a department, a division, an organization or even an industry. Consider the WorldCom scandal from several years ago. It was a fortune 500 multi-billion-dollar organization. The internal auditors asked questions about the information contained in the financial statements. Those questions led to one of the biggest frauds in United States' history.

The results of audits are not always bad. I recall performing a pay equity audit. Based on a complaint, we questioned the pay practices in one department. The audit results showed there were several individuals in a department with pay disparities. Management was unaware of the issues. When fixed, several people received a pay increase.

Questions are powerful. Internal audit reports that answer critical control questions have the power to change situations and organizations.

Finally, be prepared to do more than ask

Auditors love checklists. Many of you show up to a client site and fire off checklist questions you've obtained from the internet. But simply asking checklist questions will not get the desired results. There is more to asking questions than just asking questions. There are several techniques you must use to get people comfortable with answering questions. Auditors must be prepared to do more than just ask.

WHY IS COMMUNICATION DIFFICULT?

We were auditing the wire transfer operations in the Treasury Department of a bank. Three competent young ladies were in charge of the process. Each day, they made sure millions of dollars made it from point A to B timely and accurately.

While performing the review, we provided the treasurer with weekly status updates. The Vice President of Internal Audit was scheduled for vacation, but was pleased with the progress prior to leaving for a happy honeymoon to Hawaii.

The next week, we found an issue. While one issue may seem small, the issue itself could have had a large impact. The Treasurer as well as the three young ladies all had the ability to initiate and execute transactions without a second review. Now this meant that someone could, in theory, transfer a million dollars from one account to another without an appropriate review.

This is not normal. No individual should have the ability to release funds without review. It is important to say that just because the system allowed this activity does not mean that personnel had actually done anything wrong. Nor were we accusing them of wrongdoing. We did check several transactions to see if they were practicing proper controls with wire transfers. Thankfully there were no weird wire transfers.

We told the Treasurer. We recommended that the system setup be changed to have an adequate segregation of duties between the initiation, approval and release of wire transfers.

He disagreed.

We wondered why. There had to be some reason he wanted to have the ability to potentially do something that could cause severe damage to the organization.

The next day, the Treasurer left a copy of a memo on my desk. It was addressed to the CFO. The Treasurer accused us of accusing office personnel of stealing.

Sensing some confusion, I briefly summarized the issue in an email and forwarded it to the Treasurer. I took the time to explain that we had not accused anyone of performing unapproved transactions. As a matter of fact, it was just the opposite. No one had performed unapproved transactions. However, the system gave everyone the ability to do so.

At this point, the Treasurer doubled down and sent another letter to the CFO copying several of us with additional false claims. We attempted to schedule a meeting with the Treasurer to have a face-to-face discussion. He avoided our calls.

We then decided to meet with the CFO to inform him that there was a flaw in the system that could allow an employee to execute transactions without review or approval.

Unfortunately, the CFO was out of town traveling. We typed a memo to the CFO explaining the situation. He called the next day inquiring about the issue. Apparently, it was the first time he had heard of it. The Treasurer had not sent the CFO the previous memos.

Sending us the memos was a scare tactic. He was attempting to get us to remove the item from an audit report by threatening to inform the CFO. Not only was this embarrassing for us, but it was a waste of everyone's time.

Communication is very difficult. I think we can all agree on that.

But why?

Communication is difficult because it is

- Inescapable
- Irreversible
- Complicated

Let's explore these three items.

Communication is inescapable.
From telling the barista at Starbucks what you want, or listening to a webinar, or participating in a training course; you have to communicate with others. It is a natural part of life.

Communication is irreversible.
Once you let it out. It's out. There are no take backs. Now you have to worry about how the other party receives the message you have delivered.

Communication is complicated.
If it were easy, we would all be good at it. Osmo Wiio, a Finnish academic, journalist and author said three things about communication:

- First, if a message can be understood in different ways, it will be understood in just that way which does the most harm.
- Second, there is always somebody who knows better than you what you meant by your message.
- Third, the more communication there is, the more difficult it is to succeed.

What does this mean for auditors?
Recall the Treasurer tantrum from earlier. The Treasurer tried to avoid discussing audit issues. Rather than having constructive dialog, he chose to sling accusations and make demands through a series of unproductive memos. His tactic was to avoid the conversation in hopes that we would drop the item from the audit report. In the end, the CFO made everyone collaborate and discuss the problem.

As auditors, we need to make every effort to continuously communicate with clients. It may be easy with some and more difficult with others. Communication is inescapable.

Once we sent the memo to the CFO, we could not take it back. Unfortunately, we did not know sending the memo was unnecessary. We were honestly unaware of the Treasurer's scare tactic. But once we hit send, we could not take it back. Auditors must be careful how we communicate with clients.

And of course, communication is very complicated. We found out the Treasurer knew the system was not configured properly. The underlying issue was that he did not trust the three young ladies working for him enough to allow them to have approval authority for high dollar transactions. At the same time, he believed that the CFO would be too busy to approve the transactions.

Now, why couldn't he just say that from the beginning? It would have stopped a lot of unnecessary nonsense.

When we finally got into a room and had open and honest discussions, the CFO was okay with approving the transactions. So much wasted time for something so simple.

Communication is inescapable, irreversible and complicated.

5 Elements For Quality Questions

Many of us wish we could just crawl in a hole and never deal with another person. But we can't do that. We have to communicate to survive. Asking questions is a big part of communicating.

There are five critical elements good questions should possess. The more of these elements we have, the greater our chances of achieving effective questions.

Remember my friend Jill? She met a young man in Starbucks. They hit it off initially. Then the communication hit a plateau. Then, one bad question from her potential love interest sent everything south.

This got me thinking. Jill told me she didn't mind meeting someone and she didn't mind getting married one day. So what happened with this young man?

She told me her primary concern was that she had not known him that long. She barely knew his last name. And besides, Starbucks would not be the place to ask for her hand in marriage. Not that she was against Starbucks. The place had no significant meaning for her.

She began naming several other reasons why his question or proposal was not effective. This conversation got me thinking, what would have made the proposal effective?

And viola, the five critical elements of quality questions. Think about it, asking someone to marry you is the toughest question you can ever ask. And if we can figure out how to make that an effective question, we can tackle any other question in life.

What are the 5 Critical Question Elements?

1. Questions require a proper technique

The young man said to Jill, "Let's just go get married". There are many different ways he could have asked the question but his chosen technique did not suit her taste. Techniques will vary depending on a person's mood on a given day, the delivery style/method, and how they prefer to receive information, to name a few. You must have the right technique before you speak.

What does this mean for auditors?

While working as Director of Internal Audit for one organization, the financial statement auditors wanted to speak to me about the year-end financial statements. The firm sent some of their newer auditors to ask me what should have been simple questions.

They looked at me nervously with their clipboards and checklists in hand. The first question, "Are you aware of any significant fraud that may have occurred during the year?"

The young man raised his pen and was about to check yes or no, depending on my answer, but was caught off guard by my response.

I asked, "What do you consider material?"

He stammered and stuttered a bit and then said he didn't know. He informed me that he would have to ask the Manager and get back to me.

Next question. "Do you believe that there's any fraud in the organization?"

Again, raising his pencil because, well, who's going to admit there is fraud in the organization? He was ready for a no answer.

I said, "Yes".

He dropped his pencil in shock. His checklist did not tell him how to proceed. I began to explain to him that fraud can happen in any environment. The question is, how significant is that fraud and do we have controls in place to prevent and / or detect it?

I further went on to explain to him that I thought that there were sound internal controls in the organization, but that does not mean there is no fraud. Furthermore, there is no way that I could say there is no fraud. Internal Auditors provide reasonable, not absolute assurance.

You see, his questioning technique was terrible. He asked me a series of closed questions and became rattled when the answers didn't fit that technique.

You must have the right technique before you speak.

2. Questions must have the right audience

The young man proposed to Jill in Starbucks with a barista as the witness. I asked Jill, what would have been the right audience for her. She said it would be great for her mom and sister to witness her proposal, but while important, the audience was not a deal breaker. What I learned from this is that, while the 5 critical elements are important, the level of importance depends on the person you're asking.

What does this mean for auditors?

We were performing a review of our credit card terminals to make sure that they were in compliance with the Payment Card Industry standards (PCI). One of the requirements was that receipts should not show the entire credit card number.

We found one store with several terminals that displayed the entire credit card number on receipts. According to the corporate office, they had sent out a communication to all stores with instructions on how to correctly configure credit card terminals.

Not only was the store manager unaware of the PCI requirements, he also denied receiving any corporate communications. After spending a significant amount of time trying to communicate the concern to him, we finally gave up.

Back at corporate, we then discovered that this store had not received any PCI communications. Its credit card terminals were outsourced to a third-party provider and therefore, the store had no control over them. We obtained the contact information for the third-party provider and they fixed the issue.

Fortunately, we found out who to direct the issue to, but only after spending significant time with the store manager. While the audit issue was valid, we directed our conversations to the wrong audience.

It's important that auditors determine the appropriate parties to address concerns. Spending time explaining issues to individuals who can't make an impact is ineffective.

3. Questions must have the right timing

Jill is not a morning person. She needs her cup of coffee to wake up. Hence her daily Starbucks visits. The young man proposed to her early in the morning, when she's not at her best.

At work, we all know people who hate morning meetings. Timing may be an actual time of day, but it may also be situational. Imagine asking someone out for drinks who has been recently released from an alcohol rehabilitation program. That's bad timing.

Jill had only known the gentleman for a few hours. This was not enough time to be prepared to answer such a serious question. The timing of your questions is important.

What does this mean for auditors?

Tanya was one of the best auditors we had. She was also good friends with Rebecca, the Controller. They would go to lunch at least once a week. Most of the time their conversations consisted of life, school and studying for the CPA exam. But today, Tonya was working on an important audit and needed to talk to Rebecca.

As they were being seated, she began asking audit related questions. Looking around and seeing some competitors in the room, Rebecca's attitude soured. Tanya did not pick up on the clues and continued to ask audit questions.

Rebecca finally pulled her to the side and said, "It's not the appropriate time to ask these questions right now. Wait until the people at the table over there leave."

Timing is extremely important in most things we do in life. Just like trying to start an audit at the end of a quarter in the accounting department is a bad idea, so is discussing confidential client information during lunch hour at a popular restaurant.

Auditors must be aware of timing.

4. Questions must have the right tone

I have been unsuccessfully trying to learn to speak Spanish for years. In my most recent attempt, the concept of tone came up in the study materials. Tone is an integral part of the Spanish language. For example, if you want to declare that someone has a dog, you say:

Tu tienes un perro.
You have a dog.

This is easy. Now suppose you want to ask someone if they have a dog. You would say:

¿Tu tienes un perro?
 You have a dog?

As you can see, these phrases look very similar. And that's probably because they are. The way you distinguish between a statement and

ASK, GET, PERFORM

a question in Spanish is based on the inflection of your voice. By changing the tone of your voice at the end of the sentence, you change a statement to a question. Take a look at the Duo Lingo language learning app screenshot.

That brings us to our next critical element for quality questions. The questions that you ask must have the correct tone. Yelling at your clients can cripple your relationships, but being too meek and timid will make them lose respect for you. Therefore, the tone you choose is important.

What does this mean for auditors?

I remember working with one woman who was extremely intelligent, but her attitude was abysmal. She would constantly accuse clients of wrongdoing, oftentimes without any evidence.

I remember one walkthrough interview. She had already pulled some documentation from the system and wanted to ask more direct questions of the client.

She passed out a piece of paper with a suspicious transaction and asked, "Why did you do something so stupid?"

Staring down at the paper, I wasn't quite sure what I was looking at. At this point, neither was the client. But our auditor's tone was so bad you could sense a change in the mood of the room.

After minutes of discussion, it was discovered that someone had made a journal entry in error. The transaction that we were looking at was indeed wrong.

However, if our auditor had been a little more kind in her approach, she would have discovered the client had already corrected the issue. Instead, what happened was a 30-minute tantrum where both sides accused the other of not knowing what they were doing. Finally, everyone calmed down and resolved the issue like adults.

Tone is extremely important. Even if you think something does not look right, it's better to ask with an open mind than to question based on bias. Auditors should never badger and bully clients.

5. Questions must be asked in the right place
"Starbucks". Jill said.

She told me it would have been okay if there were some special significance with Starbucks. Otherwise, someone proposing to her in Starbucks seemed strange.

Where we experience events has special significance. Many remember where they were when certain things happened. For instance, where were you the first time you won something, were embarrassed, had your first kiss, received your first job offer. Similarly, there is a good place to ask questions.

What does this mean for auditors?
Auditors have access to all types of organizational information. Picking the proper place to disclose or discuss issues is an essential part of safeguarding your organization's information.

Therefore, we must first be aware of what type of information we're communicating. Confidential information requires a different venue than non-confidential information.

Once you've determined the type of information you need to communicate, your team should have pre planned meeting places, based on the context of the conversation.

Considering these two things prior to engaging with clients helps make a more productive conversation.

Summary

When interacting with audit clients, we must consider the 5 Critical Elements for Quality Questions.

Auditors must ask questions at the right time, using an appropriate tone, at the right place, in front of the right audience and with a good technique. Your question can be effective without all five elements. However, the more you have, the greater your chances of success.

Chapter Two

Why Ask Why?

> *He who asks a question is a fool for five minutes. He who does not ask a question remains a fool forever.*
>
> ~ Chinese Proverb

Sometimes questions annoy, sometimes they enlighten. You want to ask questions because there is power in questions.

Have you ever heard the old saying that knowledge is power? It's true. The more you know, the more you grow. But you can only obtain knowledge by being curious and asking questions. Questions give you super powers to navigate situations. The following describes the impact and power of questions.

The Power of Question

Obtain Information

I love watching suspense and crime shows. I'm intrigued by the way detectives solve crimes through questions.

The suspect is brought down to the police station. The detectives ask, "Where were you last night?"

The suspect answers. The detectives let the suspect go, research the answer, and then brings the person back to the station for more questions.

"You said you were in bed between 12 and 4 last night. However, the surveillance cameras spotted you at the local gas station at 3:35 am. Can you explain what you were doing there?"

The suspect attempts to lie again, but detectives have more evidence to show where they were. They attempt to lie yet again; the detectives have more evidence. They continue this game of asking a question, getting the answer, asking a question, getting the answer, until the suspect finally confesses.

One of the superpowers of questions is that they allow you to obtain information. Information is powerful because it leads you to a conclusion. That conclusion allows you to make sound decisions.

What does this mean for internal auditors?

Auditors should always be in pursuit of truth.

Questions lead to information; information leads to answers. Answers allow you to draw a conclusion or make a decision about a control environment, risk or process. The information you capture is critical to achieving audit objectives. Be sure to get good information by asking quality questions.

Inspire thought and creativity

Can you imagine Sir Isaac Newton sitting in the park when an apple falls near him? What happens next? His observation caused him to question why apples fall straight down instead of sideways or upward. This inspired him to develop his law of universal gravitation.

But think about this. There were probably more people in the park with him that day, but he's the only one that asked the question.

Can you imagine if Thomas Edison never asked, "Can we harness electric power and put it in a light bulb?" What if the Wright brothers never asked, "Can we build a box, put people in it and then fly?"

Questions cultivate creativity.

What does this mean for auditors?

As our profession changes, we have to develop creative solutions to be more effective and efficient in audit operations.

I remember a time when auditors would sample several transactions out of thousands to determine if activity was accurate. Many years ago, creative auditors discovered that we could simply look for duplicate transactions in Microsoft Excel.

It took a few pioneers to start the trend. Then more and more auditors began using excel in their auditing. Now auditors are doing data analysis. Some are designing dashboards for organizations. We move from traditional checkbox auditing to becoming trusted advisors. All this is happening because we are becoming creative and thinking differently.

Build Relationships and Make Connections

In his book *How to Click*, Dr. Rick Kirschner says there are three things that we know about people before they say a word.

- They love to hear themselves talk.
- They want to be heard and understood.
- They are drawn to people who listen to them.

I believe this. Who doesn't like someone that takes an interest in them? The next time you're with your friends, stop talking about yourself and start asking questions about them. They will begin to see you in a whole new light.

A simple, "How are you?" goes a long way.

What does this mean for auditors?

Oftentimes auditors approach client areas with statements. We demand to see documents; we worry about walkthroughs and everything is about placing issues in a formal report. But getting to know our clients is where fun stuff starts.

Your clients spend 8 hours a day, 5 days a week performing their processes. These processes are personal. A part of who they are professionally. We must take this into consideration when interacting with them.

There are personal things that they want to achieve in life too. Your clients have professional and personal goals they would like to achieve. If you never inquire about our clients, personally or professionally, it seems like we don't care.

If you want to build relationships with your clients, you have to ask smart questions about recent achievements in their department. You can also ask about obstacles they're facing. And finally, ask if there's anything you can do to help them. When you inquire about them openly and honestly, most people tend to open up in return. Be warned. You cannot fake it. Only inquire if you are genuine.

Coach and Mentor

In her book, *Smart Questions: The Essential Strategy for Successful Managers*, Dorothy Leeds says that when it comes to questions for coaching and mentoring, people remember best those things they discover, learn and experience themselves.

"If you want someone to digest and remember something, he has to think of it himself. The only way you help someone accept an idea as his own is to ask him a question and let him give the answer back to you."

That's pretty powerful.

She goes on to describe three questions she calls smart questions that coach.

Question 1 - What did you like about what you did?

This is a good question to ask after someone has done something. It gives them the opportunity to reflect on what they've done. And because most people dislike negativity and would prefer to talk about positive outcomes, starting with a positive is a good way to open a discussion.

Question 2 - If you could do it over again, what would you do differently?

This question not only encourages introspection but also problem solving. As I said earlier, questions have the power to inspire creativity. Asking this question might help spark that creative flame within someone. It also gives them the opportunity to address negative outcomes without direct criticism while opening the door for you to provide constructive criticism.

Question 3 - What help do you need from me?

What I like about this question is that it goes back to building relationships. If you ask this question genuinely, you end up building trust while coaching others to problem solve and think independently. It also brings things to a close nicely. The first question provides positive feedback. The second addresses room for improvement. And this question helps provide a path for going forward to implement improvements.

What does this mean for auditors?

As a leader in an audit department. It is pretty obvious that a big part of your job is mentoring and coaching audit staff. But one of my clients, Tina, taught me that the coaching and mentoring can extend to your audit clients.

Tina was the manager of a fairly large unit in an organization. Her job was to process transactions in accordance with federal laws. She had a small team, but it was not enough. They often found themselves working late nights and weekends to meet federally mandated deadlines. Everyone was stressed out.

Tina knew that there had to be a better and easier way. After some research, she found a software company that created a solution for her problem. The software cost $100,000. Tina thought this was a good deal, considering she was spending about $300,000 in temp workers and overtime.

She asked her boss for funding to purchase the software. He denied her request. Over the next several years she tried asking a few more times, only to be denied. During an internal audit of her area, we also saw the inefficient processes. The group was barely able to remain in compliance and the inefficiencies could lead to fines and penalties.

Tina told me that she had been asking her boss to purchase the perfect software solution for years. She was disappointed that he couldn't see the value in spending a little in the short term to save a lot long term.

Tina told me that she would whine to her boss once a month about the new system. I explained to her that this approach was not effective.

I then asked, "What did you like about what you did?"

"Nothing," she responded.

"If you could do it over again, what would you do differently?" I inquired.

Tina told me that she would try to find a way to get through to her boss. She realized her current method was ineffective. She suggested preparing a formal proposal, but admitted she didn't know how.

I then asked, "What help do you need from me?"

Tina asked me to help her prepare and present a proposal to her boss.

We drafted a three-page business case document. We ensured it contained enough information for her boss to make an informed decision. We practiced her pitch. She presented her case to her boss. This time, he approved the purchase.

A big part of an auditor's job is to evaluate risk, controls and processes. But along the way, there are always opportunities to help our clients by coaching and mentoring where appropriate.

Clarify situations
There are misunderstandings all the time in the communication process. Thankfully quality questions can help you clarify situations.

I remember sitting in one exit meeting with a client going over the issues. They agreed that what we had written was accurate. They also agreed to fix the issues by May. It was currently January. Four months to clear up the issues seemed reasonable.

With everyone satisfied, we wrapped up the meeting and waited to do the follow up. We contacted the client on the agreed upon completion date. The issue had not been fixed. We were confused.

We all agreed in January, that the department would have the issue resolved in May. The department director told us it was their intention to fix the item by May of next year. What caused this confusion?

Because we did not ask for clarity about the due date, we made an error in scheduling our follow up activities. Quality questions should be used to clarify otherwise ambiguous situations.

What does this mean for auditors?
Extracting information from clients and putting the pieces of the process puzzle together is extremely difficult. Organizations are multi-dimensional and several people have to work together to deliver its products and / or services successfully.

Auditors need to clarify ambiguous answers we get from clients and also clarify confusing statements we give clients.

How do you find clarity when you're confused?

First, slow down.

Now it's time to take a step back. Often we are confused about situations because we don't have all of the information. If something seems awry with clients, stop talking. Better yet, stop making statements. It's time to ask questions.

Second, attempt to find what you're missing.

Ask smart questions of your audit clients so that you can determine the point of confusion. Auditors should continuously be in the pursuit of truth. Ask clients to factually explain the situation from their perspective.

Last, follow the path provided.

We often go with our preconceived thoughts. Clarity not only requires you to seek or provide answers, but it also means being ready to accept a new path if the additional information leads in a different direction. Many people are afraid to let go of their beliefs, even when presented with factually conflicting information.

How do you provide clarity when they're confused?

First, slow down.

At this point they are most likely responding emotionally. Let them process their emotions. Don't argue or fight. Being factually right does not mean that you automatically win. After all, it is not about winning. It is about the truth.

Next, determine the point of contention.

You need to determine what your client is unclear about.

I recall one situation where we presented the client with factual evidence that something was wrong. The client began lashing out at us. Confused, I took a step back and asked if there was something wrong with the data.

Turns out, they did not trust one of my staff members. She had given them bad data at some point the past before I began working at the organization. This mistrust in her led them to discount anything the entire department delivered.

Which leads us to our last point.

Finally, evaluate the situation.

Here's a shocking revelation. Auditors can be wrong.

In the situation mentioned above, our data was good. But the interaction with the client was wrong primarily due to mistrust.

After evaluating the situation, we changed the course of this meeting. Instead of discussing the issues we walked through the data. After getting them comfortable with the data. We then discussed the issues in a separate meeting. We also discussed the department's data integrity standards. We needed to provide clarity on how we ensured data was accurate and reliable.

They were upset at something that happened before I got there. Therefore, I had to restore faith in the department's ability to analyze data and provide insight. This client's point of contention was not the issues, but more so trust in the department. Continuing to argue about issues without clarifying their true concern would have been counterproductive.

When clients are confused, it is most often an emotional reaction where you are missing something. You will need to determine the point of confusion and make corrections.

Mediating

You know it's going to be a not so fun time when you walk into a room and see audit clients sitting on opposite sides of the table scowling at one another. Although I must admit I breathe a sigh of relief when audit anger is not directed towards us.

But there is nothing worse than seeing two departments disagree over something simple. You see it all the time in organizations. Two department managers can't get along and therefore, their respective employees can't work together respectfully.

Over the years, I have developed a technique to handle situations like this. It's based on an experience I had with two dueling departments.

I remember it well. We stepped into the conference room and to find our client's fighting, each blaming the other for a failed system implementation. I had just taken a course on mediation and decided to put some of the principles to practice by asking a series of questions.

I looked at client A and asked,

"What would you like to see happen?"

Client A explained their position.

I then asked client B.

"Is this something you can do?"

Client B agreed to almost everything. There was one exception.

I then asked client A if they were okay with client B doing everything except the one item.

Client A agreed.

I then asked client B the same series of questions.

"What would you like to see done?"

Client B explained their position and conditions.

Back to client A, "Can you make this happen?"

Once they openly discussed their objectives, both determined that neither was being unreasonable. In the end, the issue was a lack of open and honest communication.

Once there was an agreement on what needed to be done, I asked the final question.

"Can we put this in writing?"

They drafted a memorandum of understanding and both parties signed the agreement. This simple mode of questioning ended a year long feud. I was thankful for that mediation course.

Questions have the power to help mediate disagreements between parties.

What does this mean for auditors?
Today's business environments are complex. Multiple people across numerous departments must cooperate to achieve goals. Unfortunately, there is a lot informal feuding that interferes with the progress of business processes.

These unnecessary rivalries can last for years. They often originate because two executives dislike one another or because someone did something to someone in another department years ago. Most times the original offenders are no longer employed with the organization. But the feud continues.

Occasionally auditors can be thrust in the middle of departmental arguments. It is important that you know how to use questions to effectively determine the truth and assist mending relationships in the organization.

Everyone knows which departments are feuding or which managers hate one another. We waste too much time and effort because of internal feuding. If you had told me years ago that a part of my job would be mediating other department managers, I would not have believed it. But over the last several years, it has been a big part of helping organizations improve.

Break through Question Barriers

There are barriers blocking you from asking good questions. Some mental, some physical. Let's talk about them. This list can help you identify and overcome them.

FEAR

I grew up without a lot. I'm not sure if I was poor, or maybe I was just too naive to notice what I didn't have. So it's no surprise that I was confused at one of my first fancy dinners with a big four accounting firm.

I was on a recruiting trip. The crowd was a mix of employees and students. I looked extremely young for my age and probably could have passed for a student.

I sat down at a table with multiple knives, spoons, forks and cups in front of me. I had no idea which utensil to grab. I didn't know which cup was mine. I had no idea where my napkin was. I immediately froze. I was afraid to ask about the arrangement. Afraid of looking foolish in front of my colleagues, or worse yet, a student.

After staring at the stemware for a few seconds, I decided, "What the heck do I have to lose." I asked the young man to my right about the table setting.

He told me that if I did not know what fork to use, he was not going to tell me. He said that we were competing for a job and this is something that I should know. The young lady on the left overheard the conversation and said, "Start from the outside and work your way in." No one had ever told me that before, but it made so much sense. I thanked her for the information.

That day, I learned not to fear looking "stupid" by asking questions. While the young man may have viewed me as foolish, the young lady did not. But at the end of the day, neither of their opinions mattered. I gained a piece of valuable information that helped me.

By the way, the young man did not get the internship, the young lady did.

Many of us are scared of looking stupid. Afraid that people might judge us, we become paralyzed with fear and don't ask questions. Fear should never stop you from asking a question that could better you as a person.

You must remember that there is no such thing as a stupid question. I like asking "stupid" questions in a room full of really smart people. I'm always amazed at how many of them don't know the answer either.

No one knows everything. Again, there is no such thing as a stupid question. However, there are questions that don't have good technique, that have a bad tone, terrible timing, or an inappropriate audience.

Does that sound familiar?

Don't ever be afraid to ask questions. Acknowledging that you don't know something and finding the answer (i.e., asking questions) is extremely intelligent. Not dumb.

UNNECESSARY ASSUMPTIONS

Working as a business consultant, companies hire you to solve problems. Oftentimes, the problems are extremely simple. The issue is typically communication. While helping organizations improve people, processes and profits, I've learned a few things.

- Assume nothing.
- Ask everything, even those "stupid" questions.

- Inquire from everyone. Almost everyone in the organization has something to contribute

There is one client that I will never forget. They pieced together several internally developed information systems to run one of their critical processes. And that process was broken.

I sat in several meetings with the software developers as they all gave their opinion about the problem. All except one.

Jackie was a petite and timid person, but the look on her face indicated she had something to say. I approached her after one of the meetings and she explained the entire problem in detail.

She had been tracking the issue for about two months. And she knew how to solve it. I began spending more time with her so that we could put together a business case to present to management.

The client's management team began to question my activities. They believed Jackie would be the last person in the world to offer a viable solution. Their assumption was based on the fact that she did not have a college education. As a matter of fact, she dropped out of high school.

What they did not know was that she dropped out at 16, primarily because she was bored and began a career as a computer programmer. She was exceptionally bright and was self-taught in eight computer languages. Not only did she know the solution to the problem, she had already tested it at home.

The management team told me privately that it never occurred to them to ask her for help. They assumed that she wouldn't know. Then they thought about times she attempted to speak up in meetings and they shut her down.

Unnecessary assumptions about others stop you from asking necessary questions. Always ask instead of assuming.

LACK OF SINCERITY

I had been looking for Joe. I had an important meeting in 30 minutes and there was something I needed to talk to him about in order to properly prepare.

When I saw him go into the break room, I rushed in behind him. He turned, somewhat startled and said, "Hi."

I responded. "How are you today, Joe?"

He spent the next 15 minutes, telling me about the things that he had been going through recently. His wife was home sick with the flu and so were the two children. At this point, it seemed to be getting worse instead of better. On top of that, his wife had a surgery schedule that she needed to cancel. Also, she had just called a few minutes ago and needed him to pick up a prescription from the store.

He then excused himself and left.

I am not a cold uncaring person, but I did not have 15 minutes to spare. But I made the same mistake most people make. By asking "How are you today, Joe?", I inquired about his health at a time when it was not important to me. I was not sincere. Most people respond to this question by saying "Okay" or "Fine". It has become something we say without thinking. Often it is not sincere.

A better question for Joe would have been, "Do you have a few minutes? I have an important meeting in 30 minutes and want to discuss something with you first."

Lack of sincerity prevents us from asking good questions. It takes effort to invest in someone else.

SITUATION ANTICIPATION

My friend Joe was down on his luck. He was a smart guy. A computer engineer. A former corporate executive. He'd been laid off from several jobs after the economy tanked.

About a year ago, he met Tammi. She was gainfully employed, and wondering when was he going to find a job?

After two years of searching, Joe finally found a job. He had just been hired as the Chief Information Officer of a company making a really good salary. He wanted to celebrate with Tammi.

Tammi entered the house from a long day at work. She could smell a pleasing aroma coming from the kitchen. The dining room table was set up like a fancy Italian restaurant. Joe was at the head of the table. He asked her to sit.

He said, "Hey, I have a surprise for you".

He pulls a box out of his pocket. It looked like a wedding ring box. Frightened at the prospect of marrying a man with no job, Tammi says, "Joe I can't marry you. You're a loser. You've not had a job in two years and I don't know if you'll ever get a job. I just need someone with more stability, more money. Someone who's gonna be there for me." Blah, blah, blah.

Joe opens the box to reveal a necklace with her birthstone. The big surprise was that he had obtained a job as a Chief Information Officer at a Fortune 500 company making a good six figure salary.

What does this mean for auditors?

We often forget to ask good questions because we prejudge situations. For example, we've all had that client with less than stellar audit results for multiple years. We then start the current year anticipating abysmal results. Similar to Tammi when she assumed the worst and began talking without context. Asking questions would have been a better option for her.

As auditors, when you are faced with situations where you don't have all of the information, ask questions instead of assuming.

UNINTENTIONAL OMISSION

A few years ago, I was in Las Vegas for a conference. I arrived a few days early, you know, for mini vacation. I saw an advertisement for a concert by a group I remembered from childhood, Blackstar. The group had broken up many years ago. They had recently gotten back together. And they were going to be performing one show in Las Vegas.

I immediately called the venue to inquire about tickets.

"Hey, listen, I'm excited about this concert," I said cheerfully to the guy on the phone.

"Me too," he replied. "This is gonna be a great concert."

"What time does it start?" I asked gleefully like a school girl about to meet her crush.

"10:30 pm. But you should get here at about 9:00 to get your tickets."

I arrived at the venue on time as promised. The tickets were sold out and had been for several months.

But how could this be? I was on the phone with a venue worker. We were just talking about the concert and he didn't tell me it was sold out.

But I didn't ask either.

He said to arrive early to get my tickets. Did he intentionally mislead me?

No. He assumed I had already purchased tickets and was wondering when I could pick them up. I assumed he was telling me when to arrive to purchase them. It was a simple case of unintentional omission.

What does this mean for auditors?
When there is confusion with client communications, don't immediately expect the worst. Most of your clients are good people and are not trying to be deceptive. Often communication issues are a simple case of unintentional omission.

The next time you think the client is withholding information or documentation, ask a few questions to clear up the confusion. It is possible you did not ask the right questions or you misinterpreted the answers.

TOO MUCH EXERCISE

Now, our final barrier to asking good questions is too much exercise. I know what you're thinking. What does exercise have to do with asking questions?

Haven't you heard the old saying that you're spending too much time:

- Dodging the issues
- Jumping to conclusions
- Beating around the bush

Summary

Asking questions is the hardest thing that you will do. It is inescapable, unavoidable, and irreversible. There is power in asking questions. But with great power comes great responsibility. That power gives you the ability to determine the truth in situations. The truth can help you improve your business and your life.

But in order to harness that power, you're going to need to break through some barriers. Some internal. Some external. You can overcome internal barriers by implementing positive principles in your life. With external barriers, it is important that you identify the cause and work with colleagues and clients to remove them.

It's not easy, but harnessing the power of questions and removing unnecessary barriers will make you a better auditor. In her book

Conversational Intelligence, Judith E Glasser says that messages miss their mark 90% of the time. That's right most of the time the person you are talking to misinterprets your message and vice versa.

I don't think people set them out to create conversations that fail. But rather, people communicate using different communication styles. When those styles align, conversations seem flawless. However, when those styles collide, they bring turmoil and chaos.

Understanding different communication styles can drastically improve the quality of your questions. Being able to relate to someone in their preferred communication style helps build a connection. The better the connection, the better you're able to communicate with colleagues and clients.

The next section is all about those communication styles.

Chapter Three

Reducing the Communication Confusion

> It's funny. All you have to do is say something nobody understands and they'll do practically anything you want them to.
> ~ J.D. Salinger, The Catcher in the Rye

We all took at least one communication course in college, so that makes us experts, right? And every incident of communication confusion we've ever faced was always the other person's fault. If only everyone else would learn how to communicate properly. Everything would be fine.

You may not have been thinking this, but it is how we act. To reduce the confusion, we need to relearn the communication process.

Back to Communication Basics

Communication typically begins with two people. Well, unless you're crazy and having conversations with the multiple personalities in your head. Otherwise, it usually takes at least two people to communicate. It's a two-way street. A give and take. A back and forth. Communication is a series of complicated processes with multiple parts moving simultaneously to make it work.

Don't believe me? Take a look at the picture below. When I ask training participants to interpret this photo, I get many different answers. Isn't it interesting how one photo can be perceived many different ways? But I will also show you there are at least nine communication concepts occurring in this one photo.

ASK, GET, PERFORM

To start, there has to be a **Sender**. Someone who has a message they want to send to someone else.

The other person is the **Receiver**.

But you don't just send a message in a vacuum. You have to choose the appropriate communication **Channel**. Some popular channels include face to face, telephone, voicemail, email, text message, Twitter, Facebook, etc. You get the point.

The sender must **Encode** the message they want to send over the chosen communication channel.

Sender — Receiver

Message

Channel

Encoding

Then there's a **Transmission**, so to speak, that takes place.

Sender — Receiver

Message
Channel
Transmission
Encoding

Once the receiver gets the message, they have to **Decode** it.

Sender — Receiver
Message
Channel
Transmission
Encoding   Decoding

Again, you have a **sender** that has a **message** that they want to send to a **receiver** over a chosen **channel**. That message needs to be **encoded**, then it's **transmitted**. The receiver then has to **decode** that message.

Recall Osmo Wiio's three points about communication:

(1) if a message can be understood in different ways, it will be understood in just the way which does the most harm.

(2) There's always somebody who knows better than you what you meant by your message.

(3) And the more communication there is, the more difficult it is for communication to succeed.

If we believe these to be true, when the receiver gets your message and begins to decode it, chances are very high that he will misinterpret the message. Now it's time for the receiver to provide **feedback**.

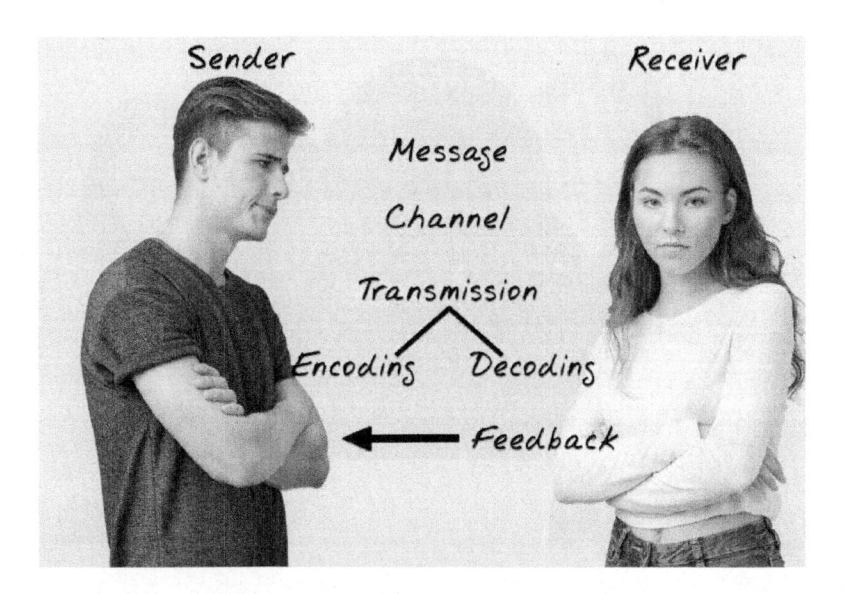

Sender · Receiver
Message
Channel
Transmission
Encoding   Decoding
← Feedback

As you're attempting to communicate, random things will pop up. These distractions come when you least expect it. They cloud the transmission, feedback, interpretation, encoding and decoding of your message. These distractions are known as **Noise**. Noise can be physical or mental.

Someone using a jackhammer outside of your office or someone screaming loudly in your home is distracting. These distractions can keep you from getting the message that someone is sending. But noise could also be the thoughts in your head. Those random thoughts are a distraction when you should be concentrating on something or someone else. Wondering about dinner plans, your significant other, that upcoming bill, etc.

You must take steps to try to reduce communication noise. That might mean clearing your head of random thoughts or finding a quiet place.

Because after all, as a sender, you want to make sure that the message you encode and transmit is decoded in a way that conveys the message you're trying to send.

As a receiver, you should want to make sure that you understand the message the sender is trying to deliver. Afterall, everything you see in page 69 is part of the communication process and happens multiple time in a matter of seconds.

That is the basic communication cycle. As you can see, there is nothing basic about it. There are several places where you will get it wrong. You might miss the message due to distractions. Because of all of these necessary steps, effective communication is a complicated process.

Moving Beyond the Basics

The objective of most audit projects is to assess risks and processes. Assessments allow auditors to conclude on the effectiveness of the risk management techniques and controls. But to truly be successful, auditors must communicate with multiple people at varying levels of authority throughout the organization.

If you think about it, our job consists of a cycle of learning and teaching. When we are assessing areas, we have to <u>learn</u> how the processes and controls function and document our understanding in workpapers. Then, we inform or <u>teach</u> management what we've learned by way of an audit report.

Because organizations and people are complex, a successful audit cycle requires being able to engage with individuals who have different communication and learning styles.

This section discusses the five communication styles, along with three learning modalities. These are designed to help us understand who our clients are, how they behave, why they behave the way they do, and what we can do to interact productively with them.

5 COMMUNICATION STYLES

THE ASSERTIVE COMMUNICATION STYLE.

Assertive is the most healthy and effective communication style.

I remember sitting in the Finance and Audit Committee meeting waiting to hear the Chief Financial Officer's status update. The Audio/Visual team was scrambling trying to prepare the microphones and the projector screen.

The ability to see and hear, were critical components for the meeting. After about 2 minutes, I heard a voice say, "Let's move forward while they continue to work on the A/V issues. Open your packets to page 57."

I had just started working for the organization, so I didn't know all the key players. I had no idea who had said this, but everyone in the room responded by following the instructions.

Her voice was commanding and steady. She logically led everyone through the prepared presentation without a microphone or PowerPoint presentation. She was concise and quick. After the update, several board members had questions. She answered all but one to the best of her ability, but promised to follow up on the one unresolved question.

This was my first encounter with an assertive accountant. She was a petite woman with a big voice. Some hated her, many feared her, but most respected her. I must admit, initially I was intimidated. She was spoken about as if she were an urban legend. Often described as cruel, cold and unkind. But as I observed her, I saw something different. She was honest and direct. She was also very factual and logical. She wasn't afraid to stand up for what was right and had no problems, respectfully, disagreeing with others.

Her assertive behavior cut through a lot of the business bullcrap you find at organizations. I learned a lot from her logical, no nonsense approach. She was by far the most effective CFO I've ever seen. Her ability to be effective is directly correlated with her assertive communication style.

How do you recognize an assertive person?

Assertive people:

- Have a moderate to high level of confidence
- Maintain good eye contact
- Encourage others to express themselves
- Actively listen to the views of others and respond appropriately
- Admit mistakes and apologize
- Have a high level of self-control
- Show appreciation for others

- Can accept compliments
- Can disagree respectfully
- Use fewer adjectives in arguments

Common phrases assertive people use.

"This was my mistake."

"I'll fix it right away."

"I will have to get back to you on that."

"Can you tell me more information so that I can understand what you were trying to say?"

"I am busy today, but we can set up an appointment for next week."

"Thank you for the suggestion. I'll consider it."

"I understand what you're saying. However, I disagree."

Here's what you can do to be more assertive.

- Maintain eye contact.
- Learn to set boundaries.
- Setting boundaries typically means learning to say no to others.

- Take ownership of your thoughts, feelings and actions
You can take ownership of your feelings by using I statements. For example, if you're upset at someone, don't say, "You made me so angry". The other person may not know that they've done something to upset you. Besides, you are responsible for your own thoughts and feelings. Instead, say, "I feel frustrated when you do…", and then describe what makes you frustrated. Express your needs and wants with confidence.
- Listen when others are speaking to you.
Listening allows you the opportunity to determine if your view is correct or incorrect.

THE AGGRESSIVE COMMUNICATION STYLE

I remember working on one audit engagement where everyone in the workplace seemed scared. I couldn't quite put my finger on it. They actually ran a tight ship. At the end of the engagement, there was only one reportable issue.

There was a new law that they were required to comply with, but failed to put proper procedures in place. We worked with the department, the attorneys and human resources to determine what needed to be done. After developing a good game plan, the department began implementing controls.

In the report we described the law and acknowledged the noncompliance, but also discussed that the department was working towards implementing a viable solution. They anticipated being in full compliance within the next three and a half months.

We (audit, legal, human resources and the department) thought this was a win for everyone. The organization as a whole, would be able to avoid noncompliance fines and penalties.

We actively communicated with the audit client throughout the engagement. Therefore, we believed the exit meeting would be uneventful. Unfortunately, we did not realize the type of personality we were dealing with.

The Senior Vice President in charge of the area came to the exit meeting with a chip on his shoulder. He explained that no area reporting to him would ever have any audit issues in an audit report. He expected perfection and any audit comments were unacceptable.

At this point we began to better understand why everyone was stressed. We had all worked in peace and harmony, without his presence. After three months of auditing, this is the first hint of animosity we had seen.

He began the meeting bullying everyone in the room. That is, until we realized we were dealing with an aggressive personality and began using countermeasures to stop his bad behavior.

You see, aggressive people are all about winning. They are extremely self-centered and care little about the people around them. They behave as if their needs are more important than everyone else's. And because he felt like one issue on an audit report reflected bad on him, he was going to bully everyone in the room to see his point of view. This issue needed to be removed.

How do you identify an aggressive person?

Aggressive people:

Speak in deceptively directive dialogue.
In other words, they do not ask questions. They bark out

commandments. This Senior Vice President told us we were going to remove the item from the audit report. It didn't matter whether he was wrong or not. People who speak in directive dialogue are exhibiting aggression.

Ask questions rudely.
You've seen people do this before. They make statement questions. In other words, they make statements, under the guise of questions. For example, suppose you are on an airplane sitting down. Someone is standing attempting to place luggage in an overhead bin. They look at you and say, "Are you just going to sit there and watch me?" This is not really a question. It's an immature cry for help.

Move close to you and invade your space.
Aggressive people are bullies. They will attempt to move close to you to push personal, physical and/or ethical boundaries. They want to make you uncomfortable so that you will succumb to their desire.

Picture that person who invites you to a surprise lunch for your birthday. Seems like a nice gesture. That is, until you pull up to a seafood restaurant. They know you don't like seafood. However, they believe you should just get over it and would like it when you give it a try. They drove, now you have no way of getting back to work. Therefore, you decide to go in and browse the menu.

What about that person who walks into your office and begins rearranging your desk because they know how to best set up your workspace? Besides, you should appreciate their superior space allocation knowledge.

Rarely show praise for your performance.
When the aggressive person decides to show praise, it will be done as a backhanded compliment. For example, suppose you cook a fairly good meal for them. The aggressive person may say, "That was a pretty good meal, however, my friend John does it better." As you can see, built into this compliment is a statement designed to undermine your efforts. If you are not careful, you will spend your time chasing compliments from someone who is incapable of giving them.

Rarely show genuine appreciation.
Similar to not showing praise, aggressive people rarely show appreciation. Almost everything is an expectation. Therefore, when you do things for them, it's because you were supposed to because of their position or grandiose beliefs.

For example, if you hold the door open for an aggressive person, they will push past without a thanks. There is no need for them to appreciate this kind act. It is what you should do simply because of who they are or what they represent.

Put you down.

Not only will an aggressive person withhold praise, but they will also find a way to criticize your performance. It is a way to help them remain in control. The desire is to make you feel bad about what you are doing, not because they truly believe you are wrong, but simply because they want you to do things their way.

Talk over other people.

What you have to say is unimportant, therefore, they will talk over you. They may also stare, glare or frown at you. Again, these are intimidation tactics done in attempts to scare or threaten you.

Things aggressive people might say.

"This is the way we've always done it and it will not change."

"I deserve this."

"You deserve this."

"Because I said so."

"Do it the way I want you to do it."

"You just don't get the way we do things here."

"You will do it one way or the other."

ROBERT BERRY

"You will do it or else."

"We'll see about that."

THE PASSIVE AGGRESSIVE COMMUNICATION STYLE.

Tina recently finished the field work on two audit engagements. She had been trying unsuccessfully for two weeks to schedule some time with each client. She thought they were avoiding her.

She peeked inside Bill's office. It was dark. His assistant told her that Bill was busy preparing for a big meeting at the end of the week. Tina continued down the corridor to Ted's office. He was sitting at his desk and appeared to be busy typing on his computer. His assistant said that he would be free around 2pm.

While heading back to her office, Tina bumped into Bill.

"I am so sorry. I received your email. However, I am extremely busy right now. I think I'm available on Tuesday. Ask my assistant to check my calendar," said Bill.

"Great," Tina said. She found Bill's assistant and setup something for next week.

At 2pm, she headed back to Ted's office. Before she could get there, Tina bumped into Ted in the hallway. "I heard you were looking for me", said Ted.

"Yes," Tina replied.

"Don't you auditors have something better to do besides stalking those of us busy working?" Ted blurted. Seeing the stunned look on Tina's face, he then added, "I'm just kidding".

Embarrassed, Ted stared at the ground, then at Tina, then at his watch. He said, "My boss is counting on me to get this report done so I need to get back to my office." Then he walked into the break room.

It was obvious Ted didn't want to talk and Tina didn't want to come off as pushy. So she headed back to her office.

In this example, Bill was assertive. He took accountability and responsibility for his actions. He had received Tina's email, but was too busy to respond. He acknowledged the issue, apologized and provided a solution.

Ted, on the other hand, was very passive aggressive. He had been ignoring her emails for weeks. Instead of acknowledging his behavior and attitude, he projected his hatred onto her. Ted has underlying issues with internal auditors. Tina is new and does not know this. Notice Ted asked if she had better things to do. This is condescending and mean.

He also didn't take accountability for his own schedule. Instead, he deflects his time management on his boss, stating that he'll be upset if he doesn't finish a report. Contrast that to Bill, who is busy as well, but took accountability for his lack of responsiveness.

How do you recognize a passive aggressive person?

Passive aggressive people are problematic. They are terrible individuals. The way they communicate seems passive on the surface, but underneath is anger and hidden resentment that comes through in subtle and indirect ways.

Passive aggressive people:

Have facial expressions that don't match their words.
They could be saying I'm sorry to you while laughing at the same time.

Frequently use sarcasm.
Notice Ted asked if Tina had better things to do, as if to say auditors don't work hard.

Inject adjectives into arguments.
You often hear them name call without explanation. For example, "Brenda in accounting is stupid." Passive aggressive people like to call people by descriptive names. It is all done in attempt to deflect you from the real issue. If Brenda is stupid, the passive aggressive person will never logically tell you why.

Use arguments from authority.

Notice how Ted blames his boss for the report being due. Passive aggressive people will blame their issues on anyone and everyone else. Many will invoke the name of God, or a boss or a spouse or a child. For example, serial killers often say God told them to kill.

Their words don't align with their actions.

If Ted was so busy and needed to get to his office, why was he going into the break room after telling Tina how busy he was?

Passive aggressive people may say some of the following.

"Oh, it's fine." - When it's really not.

"Do whatever you want." - But that's not what they mean.

"Whatever. No one cares about my opinion anyway." - This is borderline manipulation.

"Don't be so sensitive, I was only joking." - They probably weren't.

"You just take things too seriously." - After they have been overtly offensive.

"Well, I understand if you really don't want to help me. I'll suffer by myself." - The victim.

THE PASSIVE OR SUBMISSIVE COMMUNICATION STYLE

Passive or submissive people are usually counterproductive in leadership roles. Passive people want to please everyone around them. They try to avoid conflict and place the needs of others above their own.

How do identify a passive communicator?

- They have a hard time saying no.
- It's difficult for them to make eye contact.
- They have a go with the flow attitude, as if nothing matters.
- They very rarely stand up for anything.
- Their values are inconsistent.
- Their view is typically based on the view of the strongest person in the room.

Passive people may say some of the following:

"It doesn't matter. "

"Whatever you think. "

"I don't know, what do you think. "

"I want everyone to get along. "

"We'll just do whatever they want. "

THE MANIPULATIVE COMMUNICATION STYLE

Monica had been working in the Information Technology Department for over 10 years. They build and maintain computer systems for various departments in the company. She has thoroughly enjoyed her job until recently. Eleven months ago, Amber became Monica's boss. Amber brought years of experience working for organizations a lot bigger than theirs and had some new ideas she wanted to implement.

Monica did not like change. She made up her mind that she needed to get rid of Amber. That was her primary goal for next year. She set out to sabotage any chance Amber may have had at success.

It started very subtly. First, Monica would have meetings with clients and promise to deliver specific things at specific times. Next, she failed to inform Amber about the discussions. She continued to meet with the clients, pretending as though the projects were progressing on track. When deadlines were missed, she blamed Amer.

The first time it happened, Amber thought it was an accident. A simple miscommunication between two people who were new in each other's work lives. But as time passed, Amber began setting up meetings with the clients without Monica.

She noticed that clients would give a different story from that told by Monica. For example, Monica told her that there were no outstanding items with one client, but when Amber met with the client, they had a list of items that required correction.

Monica was slowly attempting to manipulate relationships. She wanted Amber gone and it was obvious that she was doing everything in her power to make that happen. Amber felt frustrated because she could not get straight answers from Monica. Thankfully, talking to the clients directly cleared up many of her concerns.

Eventually, Amber confronted Monica. Of course, Monica denied everything. Amber began to work more closely with Monica. She would invite her to joint meetings with clients. With everyone in the same room, it became difficult for Monica to manipulate the situation.

In her attempts to get rid of her boss, Monica wanted to manipulate people. In the end her plan failed and she ended up without a job. I said earlier that passive aggressive people were problematic but manipulative communicators are monsters. They are the worst people on the planet.

How do you identify a manipulative person?

They spend a majority of their time being secretive
You must watch out for this type of person. You know them when you see them. They are the keepers of secret gossip. They confide in you and encourage you not to interact with others. But you're not special. They are doing the same thing to others. They make you feel special. Like you are part of the popular group. Truthfully, you are simply a pawn in their dirty chess game.

They are the catalyst for confusion
In our story above, both Amber and her clients were confused about the status of projects. That is because Monica was behind the scenes manipulating situations. Confusion prevents you from discovering the truth. The more confusion, the longer it takes to solve problems.

They secretly influence others without regard for the greater good
Monica was willing to let the projects fail because her desire to get rid of her boss was of greater concern than the success of the department.

Manipulative people are self-centered
They feel the need to control others to get the outcome they desire. What they desire may not be in the best benefit of the most people.

Manipulative people are dishonest

They lie so good that they actually start to believe the lies they tell. They lie without remorse because to them the ends justify the means

They are filled with emotion

Manipulative people behave the way they do because some emotion is guiding them. Guilt, resentment, irritation, anger. Some emotion is causing them to behave the way that they're behaving. Their emotions are typically on extreme ends of the spectrum. If you are a pawn in their scheme, they will be extremely nice. If you are the object of their anger, they will be extremely mean. But beware, once the manipulation is over, the manipulative person will no longer need you.

These people are completely destructive and scum of the earth. They are not to be trusted at all. There are no redeeming qualities for manipulators.

Manipulative people say some of the following.

It is very difficult to pinpoint and describe the manipulative mind of these people. Their tactics vary and encompass many of the things that you see from the aggressive, passive aggressive, and passive person. They are truly a mixed bag of tricks. When you find one, you need to avoid them. Combating them is pointless. They have no shame and no values. But they do have a lot of emotion. That emotion leads them to do things that make no sense. Therefore, the manipulative person is willing to do things that most people won't in order to accomplish their goals.

3 LEARNING STYLES

At this point, you're probably wondering why learning styles are in a book about asking questions while auditing. Think about it like this:

- The primary purpose of our job is to ask a lot of questions to learn about client's processes.
- After we learn, we then evaluate processes to determine if they are effective, efficient and in compliance with laws, rules and regulations.
- Finally, we create reports explaining (or teaching) clients what we found.

That means auditors are learners and teachers. Just like there are different communication styles, there are different learning styles. It is important for auditors to present information to clients in a way that best meet your clients' preferred learning styles.

The most common learning styles are the VAK.

VAK learning styles form a model of learning designed by Walter Burke Barbe and later developed by Neil Fleming. The VAK model helps you understand and explain a person's preferred or dominant thinking and learning style. The principle behind the VAK model is that people are either Visual, Auditory or Kinesthetic.

That means people experience, learn, communicate and interact based on what they see (visual), what they hear (auditory) or what they experience (kinesthetic).

Learning Style	Description
Visual	Likes seeing and reading
Auditory	Likes listening and speaking
Kinesthetic	Likes touching and doing

VISUAL LEARNERS

The visual person is known to be organized, neat, and orderly. A good speller. Memorizes by seeing pictures and less distracted by noise. The visual person may also have trouble remembering verbal instructions. Their mind wanders with too much verbal.

When communicating with this person, you need to show them pictures. These are the people that need to see your flowcharts instead of talking about the process. They like to see graphs and numbers. They love red, yellow, green dashboard.

AUDITORY LEARNERS

Typically, auditory people talk to themselves, are easily distracted once engaged, move their lips when they're reading and find math and writing more difficult. Spoken language is easier and they tend to like music.

This is the audit client you'll be able to have a conversation with without the flowcharts.

KINESTHETIC LEARNERS

The kinesthetic person responds to physical reward. They touch and stand close to people. They also tend to move a lot and typically have a larger physical reaction to things. They learn by doing, point when reading and respond physically to people.

This is the audit client that you talk to about the process but they don't understand. You show them the flowchart, they still don't understand it. But if you take them by the hand and walk them through the process, they get it.

What are some indicator words to identify learners?

Your clients are visual, auditory, and / or kinesthetic. Some want to see flowcharts. Others want to read narratives. While some just need for you to walk them through the processes. All in all, they need for us to see it, say it, and experience it.

Here are some common indicator words and /or phrases for the different learning modalities. Use it to help you determine how to communicate with clients and colleagues.

Figure 1 - VAK Indicator Words / Phrases

Visual	Auditory	Kinesthetic
I see what you're saying.	I just want to be heard.	He couldn't catch on to the joke.
Let's make this as clear as possible.	That rings a bell.	Let's tap into her experience.
I can't imagine….	It's falling on deaf hears.	We need a complete turnaround.
From my point of view….	Sounds like we all agree	Let's get a handle on the situation.
Her words were foggy.	I'm all ears.	Get a hold of yourself.
This is what I envisioned.	Let's make music together.	I was hoping she would catch on.

Chapter Four

5 Step Approach to Quality Questions

> *Life is like a multiple-choice question. Sometimes the choices confuse you, not the question itself.*
>
> *~ Anonymous*

Throughout this text I've been saying that communication is a fluid and complicated process. You may be wondering; how can I boil it down to a five-step approach. You've also heard me say that mechanical methodologies won't necessarily work, and yet here I am talking about the 5 Step Approach to Quality Questioning. It is a baseline methodology with flexibility and fluidity built in. It is the cornerstone of the quality questioning concept.

Up to this point, I have said

One, questioning is the hardest thing that you will ever do.

Two, there is power in asking questions, and we need to harness the power that questions possess.

And three, there's more to asking questions than just asking questions.

The art of asking questions is complex. There is not a single checklist that can make you a better question asker. There is, however, a methodology that ensures you have the appropriate tools to navigate most situations.

Before you ask a single question, you need to be able to collaborate with the other party. There needs to be some sort of relationship. Establishing relationships requires you to understand various auditor and client personality types.

Because the communication process is crazy confusing, at some point you or your clients will take things out of context. Therefore, it is important for auditors to identify situations in which providing or obtaining context can clear situations up.

Now that everyone is one the same page, you must use the appropriate questioning technique.

You can try hard to reduce the communication confusion, but you will almost always have to provide or seek clarity in conversations.

And finally, you must make a commitment to continuously have construction communication with your colleagues and clients.

Those are the components to the five-step methodology. Let's talk about each of them.

Figure 2 - 5 Step Approach to Quality Questions

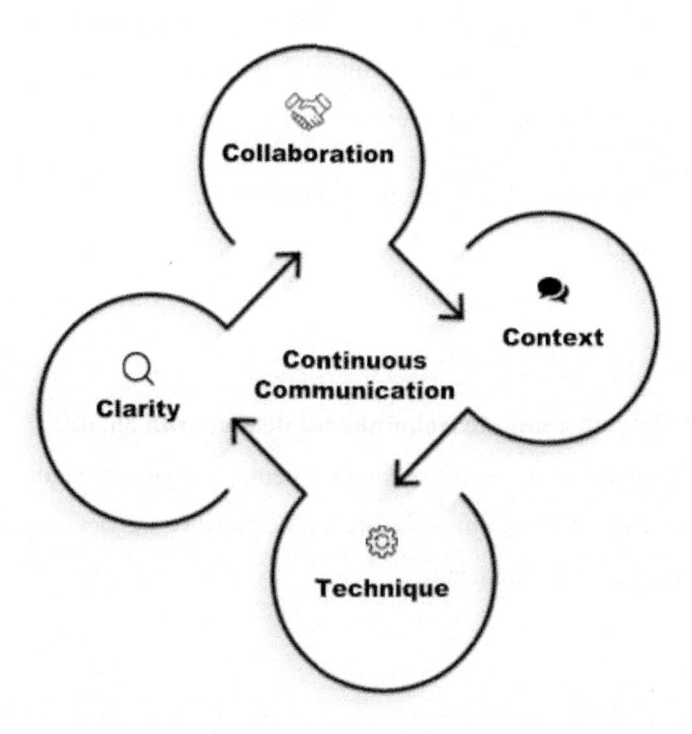

- Collaboration
- Context
- Clarity
- Continuous Communication
- Technique

Step 1 - Collaboration is Key

Let's talk about collaborating with audit clients. To effectively collaborate with clients, you must take responsibility for your role in the communication process. The following are three ways to take responsibility for your role in the communication process.

First, understand your personality as an auditor.

As auditors, we exhibit certain personality traits. Some good and some bad. If we have a good understanding of our personality, we can capitalize on the strengths while also reducing the weaknesses within the various auditor personality styles we have.

Second, understand your clients' personalities.

We must understand client personalities so that we can improve inherent weaknesses and capitalize on strengths in the various personalities.

Third, develop a unique technique for dealing with clients.

The technique should be tailored to the client, taking the strengths of our personality and the strengths of their personality and developing a collaborative environment.

UNDERSTAND YOUR AUDITOR PERSONALITY

There are at least four personality types you'll see in auditors. I can guarantee that each us has fallen into one or even all four categories at some point in our career.

THE ARROGANT AUDITOR

You've seen them. You know the ones who go into audit engagements talking about how terrible the client is. They've audited the client for the last five years and they know everything there is to know about the department and the department is terrible. Further, if the client would only listen to them, they would be better off.

Now mind you, there's a difference between giving your audit staff a heads up on client's culture, versus downright arrogance. Typically, your arrogant auditor will tell you how bad or good the department is and go in with a laser sharp focus trying to confirm what they believe (good or bad). No one is immune from exhibiting this auditor personality. We can become accidentally arrogant. Thinking we are helping the situation; we behave in a manner that is outside of our normal character.

If you are an arrogant auditor, you miss out on the opportunity to do three things.

Learn something new.

Every time we go into a department it's a learning experience, even if you've audited them before. The arrogant auditor is not objective and believes there is nothing new for her to learn.

Connect with clients.

Most of your clients are wonderful people. We should all work together to achieve organizational goals and objectives. Truly connecting with clients allows you to collaborate to contribute to building a better organization.

Serve your clients.

Our job is to take an objective look at client operations so that we can provide stakeholders with some reasonable assurance that controls are either functioning as intended or not. If you have an arrogant attitude, you'll never be able to accomplish that goal. Clients will not trust you and you will not be able to perform well.

You have your outright arrogant auditors. But what about those who are accidentally arrogant?

I know that sounds strange. You may think there is no such thing as being accidentally arrogant. But let me give you an example. At one point in my life, I changed careers. I moved from financial services to higher education. I entered the higher education industry as a Director of Audit. I had no idea what the industry was really like. As a result, I had a lot of catchup work to do.

I studied the industry. I went to training courses, had a lot of conversations with audit clients, read a lot, etc. Thankfully, one of my first projects was working with the organization in reviewing the new purchase card program.

We were dealing with a lot of banks. Whoo Hoo, that was right up my alley. It was something that I was familiar with. And my clients trusted me in this process. They invited me to a lot of meetings. I noticed that in those meetings because I had a lot of knowledge about the banking industry, I was doing a lot of talking. But at some point, I think maybe I was doing a little bit too much talking. I should have been asking more questions, so that I could get better answers, so that I could perform better audits

But I was very excited because I was comfortable. I felt at home. But this could come off as a bit arrogant. They invited me there as a casual observer. A trusted advisor. I wasn't there to control the process. I was there to ensure that proper controls are in place. As I've said before, curiosity is the cornerstone of internal auditing. And at that particular point in time, I wasn't being very curious.

I remember sitting in one meeting and I could hear myself. Then it hit me. I said to myself, "Shut up." And with that, I started getting back on track.

Whether you have outright arrogant auditors, or accidentally arrogant auditors, you need to squash that immediately.

Here are three characteristics of arrogant auditors.

You talk more than your client.

If you talk more than your audit client, you might be an arrogant auditor.

You don't ask questions.

Now, mind you, there's a difference between asking questions and questioning people. For example, if you're asking a question, you might say to an audit client, "How did this happen?" or "Can you help me understand the process that led up to this?"

Now, if you are questioning people you might say, "How could you let this happen!" You see, there's a difference.

You don't communicate to understand.

There's not a commitment to trying to understand what's going on. You simply want to give orders and make directives. But you cannot lead until you understand the situation.

If you find yourself acting like this, whether on purpose or accidentally, there is hope.

Here's what you should do if you find you are an arrogant auditor.

First, shut up.

Just be quiet. It's just that simple. If you find yourself talking too much, be quiet.

Second, listen to your clients.

Open your ears. Really hear what they are saying. If you recall the retail store incident from earlier. We did really good work uncovering fraud. But we didn't listen enough to understand the client's ulterior motive. He wanted to clear his friend's name. Had we known this, we would have approached the situation with the client differently.

Third, practice being sincere.

Sincerity should not be faked. But arrogant individuals seem to only care about themselves. With patience and practice, you can get over yourself.

So, are you an arrogant auditor? Only you can answer that question. But I can't tell you that even if you think you're not, at certain points in time, you will exhibit arrogant behavior. It's in all of us.

APPREHENSIVE AUDITOR

Are you an apprehensive auditor? I remember the first time I realized I was an apprehensive auditor. It was early in my career. The engagement manager sent me to interview a Senior Vice President in an organization by myself. I remember walking down the long executive hallway in the multi-billion-dollar organization. The hallway was filled with paintings of people who founded the organization and other expensive art pieces. It was intimidating.

He was in a huge corner office overlooking the river. It was bigger than my apartment. His assistant led me into his area. As I entered the room, I could see him sitting behind a huge desk made of mahogany wood. He turned to face me. And I came face to face with this stout man with a deep voice. He invited me to sit. His chairs were nicely padded and plush. The kind that made you want to fall asleep immediately after sitting down.

I explained to him that I was there to ask a few questions about the operations. He gave me one of those "Why are you wasting my time?" looks.

And at that moment, in a split second, my confidence slipped. I felt fear taking over my body. I became apprehensive to ask even the most basic questions out of fear of looking stupid in front of this man. I'm sure you've been there before. Panicked and paralyzed. Afraid of speaking up. Afraid of speaking out.

What are some characteristics of an apprehensive auditor?

Nervousness

You become nervous out of fear. You must work to remove negative thoughts that keep you stuck.

Negative self-talk

While in the SVPs office, I was continuously subconsciously saying to myself, "I can't ask him that question. He might think I'm stupid". This negative self-talk prevents you from doing your job primarily because it leads to fear.

Fear

We all fear something. Throughout our lives we spend time identifying and overcoming fears. I can remember playing American football. The first time I hit someone was fun and fearful at the same time. But with a little practice, I became good at it.

I remember the first time I rode a bike by myself. I was afraid of falling. The first time I fell, I was very apprehensive to ride again. But I did. I got better and better. Eventually I was jumping on ramps, riding on one wheel and doing all kinds of stuff I never thought I'd do.

If you find yourself being an apprehensive auditor, here's what you can do.

First, be prepared.
When I walked into the SVP's office, I was actually prepared. I knew my stuff. But I let the negative self-talk get to me. I became afraid of what he might think. Adequate preparation can put you on the right path. But preparation alone is not enough.

Next, realize that the person you are talking to is only human.
The person you feel puts their pants on one leg at a time just like you. They know some things that you don't know. And you know some things that they don't know. They may have more money than you or they may have less. None of these things make them better than you. We are all human and have jobs to do. Doing your best on the job should be your primary objective.

Finally, don't worry about the worst-case scenario.
You might embarrass yourself, but it's okay. You can always make a comeback from embarrassment. Or the outcome could be positive. What's the worst that could happen? You can bounce back from anything short of death. Besides, our deepest fears rarely come true.

Summary

If you're an apprehensive auditor, you might be nervous. You might have some negative self-talk. If you want to overcome that, you must be prepared, realize that they are only human and don't worry about the worst-case scenario.

THE PUSHOVER AUDITOR

If you're not arrogant or apprehensive, you might be a pushover. This is the absolute worst. But we've all been there. When you are a pushover, a few things will happen.

- **You won't get the information that you need** from your audit clients. Which means
- **You won't be able to do Job.** Which could mean
- **You might not have a job for long.**

You've seen pushover auditors. They ask clients for information, documentation or meetings, but typically tend to have problems getting what was requested. This is a bad place to be in.

It's important to remember that the pushover is usually not a permanent situation. You may be in this position with only one client that makes you nervous. Not every client will like you. However, if you find that you have these issues with a majority of your clients, there could be a problem.

If you are a pushover, here are four things that you can do to overcome the condition.

First, remove your fear.

I get it, you are afraid to ask questions because you don't want to be judged. Manipulative people feed into your fear. They may tell you, "That was a dumb question". It is a terrible tactic designed to attack your self-confidence.

But remember, there is no such thing as a dumb question. The moment you realize this, you can overcome our fear of asking questions and interacting with clients.

Second, determine and get what you need.

The problem with Pushovers is that they often do not know what they need and/or how to get it. The best and only way to determine what you need is by asking questions. Determining how to get it involves interacting with various personnel. Some may be cooperative, while others may be difficult.

Third, set firm due dates and expectations

People push past your boundaries and ignore your expectations because you either 1) do not have any or 2) have not communicated them. Most people are not terrible humans who purposely ignore your needs. Therefore, it is extremely important to set expectations with clients.

Fourth, do not fear escalation.

If sufficient time has passed and you've not received what you need, it may be time to escalate the issue. Before doing this, you must determine your department's escalation procedures. If your department does not have escalation procedures, that is a problem. Your managers have not equipped you with the tools you need to succeed.

Again, obtaining adequate information and documentation is one of the biggest hurdles that pushover auditors face. The way to conquer that is to set appropriate expectations with clients and utilize your department's information escalation process.

THE COMFORTABLE AUDITOR

Our last audit personality type is the Comfortable Auditor. This is where we want to be. These are the auditors who have eliminated their arrogance. They're not apprehensive because they prepared and they're not pushovers.

This is very difficult to attain because clients and environments change. Change brings uncertainty. Uncertainty interrupts our comfort zone. Therefore, we all navigate between one of these four auditor types throughout our career.

Here's what you need to do to be the comfortable auditor.

Eliminate arrogance.

As mentioned, we all can fall into the accidental arrogant phase. We've all acted in a manner that was grandiose. But good people can recognize changes in their behavior. And if you do not recognize it, the comfortable auditor can at least acknowledge when someone informs them they are acting in a manner that is the opposite of their core character. Unfortunately, if you are always arrogant, this tip will not help you.

Try not to be apprehensive.

Make sure that you've adequately planned for audit engagements and get as much training possible so that you know what you're talking about.

Interact with audit clients.

The more we interact with our audit clients, the more comfortable we'll be around them, and the more comfortable they'll be around us. Make sure that your clients see you outside of audit engagements. I'll talk about this more later.

Don't fear failure.

Negative self talk stops us from achieving our goals.

Have you said or thought any of the following?

"I can't talk to the CFO, he may discover I am inadequate."

"I can't ask the client this stupid question. I should know this already."

"They will think I'm incompetent if I ask this question again."

This negative self-talk only ensures that you will not achieve your goals. Don't fear failure. If you fail at something, pick yourself up and start all over again. Life is all about second chances. If we want to be comfortable as auditors, we have to realize that sometimes we will fail.

UNDERSTAND AUDIT CLIENT PERSONALITIES

Prior to becoming an auditor, I never dreamed that a big part of my job would be managing people's emotions. But it is. And talking to others in the profession, it appears as though I'm not alone. So let's talk about the various audit client personality types that you might encounter and how to collaborate with them.

THE DETACHED CLIENT

I once worked for a fairly large multi-billion dollar organization. We had offices in a central part of the city and five other states. The local corporate campus was huge and was where a majority of the employees worked. It was on the south side of the city close to the interstate. The CEO, however, had solo office space downtown overlooking the river, 10 miles from the rest of us.

Getting in touch with him was fairly difficult for those without superstar status in the organization. His office space was detached from the rest of the company literally and figuratively. This detachment trickled down to many of the other managers.

What happens when you have a detached audit client?

- Oftentimes management is unaware of what happens at lower levels.
- The lines of communication are broken.
- Processes don't line up with business objectives.
- There always seems to be incomplete information floating around.

Your client might be detached if:

Employees cannot clearly communicate goals and objectives.
When your clients are detached, there's a disconnect in the communication. There is a gap between upper management's expectations and employee's understanding of those expectations.

The client is difficult to reach.
Every organization has a set of communication protocols. But those protocols should never be counterproductive. In the organization I mentioned previously, there were oftentimes issues that required the CEO's attention, however, scheduling meetings with him took months. This is because the CEO was detached.

The client is not responsive to audit staff.
Responsiveness does not mean fulfilling our every request. It does mean being honest and timely with responses. The detached client becomes a big problem for the Pushover Auditor. A detached client is very detrimental not just to the audit process, but to the entire organization.

How do you overcome the detached audit client?

Try to get close.
Now I don't mean stalk them. Strike up some conversations based on common interest. One common interest you have is the success of their department. So start there.

It does not have to remain professional. You may have some personal interest in common. For example, I love ice cream. I worked for an organization that actually had an ice cream club. The first Tuesday of every month we had ice cream "management" meetings.

Getting close can be professional, personal or both. Either way, getting close helps overcome the detached audit client.

Be a problem solver
When I was a kid, I could fix almost any desktop. Because of this, my friends would ask me to repair their computers. Sometimes I

would help and other times I would refuse. My willingness to help would be based on the way they approached the situation.

One friend, let's call her Tammy, would drop her computer off and simply say, "I broke my computer, can you fix it?" The first time she did this, I fixed it. The second time, I refused.

Now let's take my other friend Steve. Steve would drop his computer off and he would say, "My computer's broken. I was last in Microsoft Word. I hit control-alt-delete and the screen went blank. I researched some of this on Google and I think it could be..." and then he would rattle off a couple of things that he thought could be the problem.

My grandfather used to have a saying. If you want my help bring me solutions, don't bring me problems. With Tammy, I would have no clue where to start. The difference between the two is that Steve would offer some potential solutions. He would also explain how he got into the situation he was in. in other words, he gave me enough information to be of assistance to him.

It's the same approach with our audit clients. If you are simply presenting a problem to the client, it may not be well received. But if you detect a problem, do some preliminary research and actually engage with the staff to come up with some solutions. Now the issues you present are less burdensome. Bring your clients solutions as often as you can.

THE COMBATIVE CLIENT

I was fairly shocked the first time I ran into a combative audit client. We were doing an information technology review of network access. We noticed several vulnerabilities that would have left the organization's information exposed to hackers.

We discussed the issues with management and drafted an audit report. On the day of the exit meeting, I could see and hear some of the client personnel walking down the hall in front of us.

One of them said that he had no problems with the audit report and the issues were good. He also said that they needed to fix them, however he was going to argue with us in attempts to get us to remove items from the audit report.

Hearing this helped put my mind at ease. We were almost certain that the issues were accurate. During the exit meeting, he attempted to argue. Confident in the work that we had done, we didn't argue, we didn't fuss and we did not fight. This was clearly an example of a combative client. He wanted to argue simply for the sake of arguing

Your client might be combative, if they:

- **Try to intimidate, harass, or scare their own personnel.**
- **Try to intimidate, harass or scare audit personnel.**
- **Continuously argue without sound reason.**

What to do when you encounter a combative client?

Don't match their tone.

If they're acting like a kid, don't stoop to their level.

Remain calm.

When you're all riled up, you start to become apprehensive. Or worse, a pushover. Remain calm. What's the worst that could happen?

Stick to the facts.

What's happening is you're bringing them something that they don't want to hear and they're giving you a defensive response.

As an auditor, you're simply delivering the news. People oftentimes try to shoot the messenger when the news is bad. But you didn't cause or contribute to the problem. Always remember that. You are simply delivering information. Stick to the facts.

THE MAGICAL CLIENT

You've seen the magician before. The audit starts and you request information from them. You've taken proper precautions to ensure you aren't infringing on their time. They tell you everything is a go and they'll have the information and people lined up for you in a few weeks.

You go off and do other things so that your client can prioritize their workload. You come back on the agreed upon date and time. And nothing. They claim they had everything ready to go but they got swamped. Or someone misplaced it. You try to be understanding. Things happen in life. But a heads up would have been nice.

Or what about when you identify a person you need to speak with because they are critical to a process. The magician tells you that you cannot speak to them this week because they are busy closing the books. You agree to not disturb anyone this week and to come back next week. When you visit the office the next week, the person you need has magically disappeared. Maybe they're on vacation, maybe they got fired. But all you know is that they just disappeared. And again, no warning from your client.

Here are some things magical audit clients do.

Bury you with paper.

They believe if they give you a ton of paperwork, they can hide what's really going on. Bernie Madoff is said to have done this to auditors.

Make certain personnel and / or paperwork just disappear.

So either they give you too much or they don't give you what you need at all. That's your magician.

Provide extravagant dinners, lunches, or maybe even free tickets to shows.

In a recent discussion with the University of Cambridge's Master of Accounting class, Sam Antar, former CEO of Crazy Eddie described how he manipulated auditors. He used gifts and other incentives to distract them from conducting decent audits.

His tricks allowed the company to commit fraud for decades. Eventually, most family members were sent to prison for their role in the fraud.

Here's what you can do to overcome the magical audit client.

Take the extra paperwork

For those who try to give you extra stuff, go ahead and accept all that information. You can sort through it later. You know what you really need. If it is not easily accessible, you'll have to ask for assistance. Don't bear the burden of hunting too long for something that doesn't exist. This puts the responsibility back on the client. Everyone's goal should be to complete the audit as efficiently as possible. And these tactics are counterproductive. Do not get bogged down by them.

Second, go on a scavenger hunt.

There may be someone else in the organization that can provide the information you need. Do not spend a significant amount of time on your hunt. If it fails to produce results in a reasonable time, you may need to escalate.

Third, reject those extravagant gifts. They are distractions.

Or if you do accept them, ensure you adequately disclose everything to the appropriate person in your department in charge of monitoring conflicts of interest. The transparency takes away perceived bias.

CONFIDENT CLIENT

This type of client understands the audit process and is comfortable talking to and interacting with you.

I actually have had a lot of clients that fall into this category. But both you and your client's have to put in a lot of work to get there. You can't blame clients for every audit debacle. You have a role to play in developing relationships. Tools and techniques presented here should help you do your part.

Comfortable clients equates to more productive, collaborative and insightful projects.

How do you move your clients from cautious to being comfortable?

That's a big task. Simply being smart does not get you there. Clients don't care how much you know, until they know how much you care.

There are three things that you can do to move your clients from cautious to comfortable.

- First, show them that you care.
- Second, show them that you're competent.
- Third, let them in on the process.

1. Show them your care

You can show your clients that you care by:

Visiting them periodically.
Auditors should not be confined to cubicles. You should be up walking around, visiting your clients. And not just when it's time for an audit. The more they see you, the more clients become comfortable with your presence. The more you engage, the more they believe you care. It shows that you're in it with them.

Inquiring professionally
If you know that a client is working on a tough or an exciting project, ask them about it. If a client is trying to cope with new regulatory changes, ask them about it. Remember what Dr. Rick Kirschner said in his book *How to Click*, people like to hear themselves talk. People are drawn to people who are drawn to them. While you are at it, ask if there is anything you can do to help them.

Inquiring personally
You don't always have to do this. Sometimes it's uncomfortable. And it may not be effective with all clients. But if there's a client that you really like, and you want to know how they're doing personally, ask them.

People love it when others genuinely care about them. So show your clients that you care.

2. Show them you're competent

How do you prove to people you know what you're doing?

The following are three steps you can take to begin showing clients that you are confident.

- Study their business
- Study your craft
- Let them in on the audit process

Study their business.

Companies today are becoming more and more complex. I spent a large part of my career in higher education. It was an eye opening experience. I needed to know a little about a lot of industries. Think about it, a campus is like a mini city. There are dormitories, food venues, fitness centers, law enforcement agencies, research, grants, technology and more.

There is no way to know everything, but you need to study their business. It's our job to know a little bit about a lot of different things. You should be reading a lot of trade publications and going to conferences. Ask them what trade journals they subscribe to. Get copies of the journals when they are finished. There are a variety of things you can do to study your clients business. I have even attended nonaudit related training alongside audit clients. That's right. I have been to training with some of my clients.

Study your craft as an internal auditor.
Look at the standards, read the standards, and know the standards. You will almost never be able to be an expert at something your client does eight hours a day, seven days a week. But you better be an expert auditor.

I remember working in one audit department where many of the auditors had never read the standards. And these were not new auditors. That does not make sense. Needless to say, I did not fit in well with that group. To be a proficient auditor, you need to read, attend training, and be aware of audit trends and techniques.

Let them in on the process
The audit process should not be a secret. Clearly explain internal audit to your clients. Next, explain your department's processes. Finally, reiterate these things as much as possible.

Tell them what you do. Tell them how you do it. The more they hear it and the more they see you acting it out, the more believable it is. So don't keep your processes secret from your clients.

Conclusion

There you have it. In order to collaborate with your audit clients, you need to first take a look at yourself. Understand your personality. Then, you need to understand the various client personality types. After that, create a technique for relating to clients based on the personalities of the people in each area.

Step 2 Don't Get Taken Out of Context

No matter how hard we try, there will always be points of confusion in the communication process. Regardless, we must try to be as clear and concise as possible.

Context is critical in conversations. Remember what Osmo Wiio said. Most people will interpret what we say in the way that does the most harm.

I believe that this is amplified for auditors. We deliver news to clients. Sometimes the news is good, other times it's bad. When bad, we run a high probability of upsetting our clients. And that is why context is so important.

Now I know what you're thinking, you would never take anything out of context. You're a kind and patient person who always listens to everyone. But I'm here to tell you that the out-of-context disease can affect anyone.

Take, for example, common phrases we say every day without proper context.

Have you ever heard the phrase, money is the root of all evil?

People toss this phrase around all the time. Anti-capitalists often use this phrase in attempts to prove that capitalism is bad.

But did you know this is not the actual quote? After hearing this phrase my entire childhood, I did not discover the correct quote until I was in my thirties.

It comes from the Bible, 1st Timothy Chapter 6 verse 10.

"For the love of money is a root of all kinds of evil. Some people, eager for money, have wandered from the faith and pierced themselves with many griefs."

This context changes the commonly accepted meaning of the phrase.

First, money is not the root of all evil. According to the correct phrase, the love of money is the root of all kinds of evil. You can have money and not be in love with money. But take a look at the second sentence. People eager for money "pierced themselves with many griefs." According to this, the people chasing money, not necessarily the ones with money, have problems.

Now that we know the truth, how many of us have misquoted and/or misinterpreted this quote?

Most misunderstandings are simple mistakes. There are, however, some who use confusing context as means to manipulate situations.

What can you do if context is a concern?

Calm down before you respond.

Overreacting to a situation is a surefire way to make it worse. Take a few deep breaths and think about the situation you are in.

Give your client your full attention.

There's nothing worse than having your client pour their heart out and you act as if you don't care. Even if you are right, there's still work to do to get everyone on the same page.

Remember that you don't have to respond

Sometimes clients just want to vent. Venting is emotional. While in this state, things clients say may be emotional, but not accurate. You do not have to respond. This is most likely a temporary state. Correcting them at this point may make the situation worse.

If you decide to respond, remember questions have the power to coach and mentor. People tend to buy into ideas that are their own. By asking thoughtful questions, your clients can move from emotional to rational. So before you respond with advice, ask questions.

Be open to alternative outcomes.

Oftentimes when we interact with others, we have specific outcomes in mind. But we may be jumping to conclusions prematurely. Calm down, pay attention to your clients, remember you don't have to respond and be prepared for the unexpected.

STEP 3 - CHECK THE TECHNIQUE

Mark Zuckerberg, CEO and founder of popular social network website Facebook, was called to testify before Congress. Senator Dan Sullivan asked the CEO what he, the Senator, thought was a simple question. Zuckerberg's unexpected answer caught the Senator off guard. Here's the dialog:

Sullivan: Mr. Chairman, Mr Zuckerberg. Quite a story right? Dorm room to the global behemoth that you guys are. Only in America would you agree with that?

Zuckerberg: Senator mostly in America.

Sullivan: You couldn't do this in China right? What you did in ten years.

Zuckerberg: Well senator there are some very strong Chinese internet companies.

Sullivan: Right but you're supposed to answer yes to this question.
Okay come on...
I'm trying to help you...
All right...
I mean, Give me a break.

> You're in front of a bunch of...
>
> The answer is yes.
>
> Okay, so thank you.
>
> Now, your, your testimony...

Check out the video here (https://youtu.be/SEWeOIX5SEE).

You see, Zuckerberg is a multi-billionaire. The Senator asks him if his story is so unique that it could only happen in America. The Senator became frustrated when the Facebook CEO did not simply answer yes. To make the matter worse, the Senator did not allow Zuckerberg to actually answer the question.

This is an example of poor questioning technique. The Senator wanted to make a point based on his belief that Zuckerberg has done something quite unusual and unique to America. Zuckerberg obviously did not share that same sentiment and therefore did not answer as expected. The Senator would have been better off making a statement about his belief.

But it doesn't stop there. He attempts to shame Zuckerberg by saying the following:

"All right. I mean, Give me a break. You're in front of a bunch of..."

He's implying that Zuckerberg should comply with his bad question because he is in front of a bunch of Washington elites. Never mind the fact that the Senator is wrong. But we'll touch on that a little later.

This shows not only a poor choice of question type, but also poor timing, bad place, wrong audience.

Sound familiar?

When we ask the wrong questions, we don't get the information we need. Additionally, we waste time and money on wild goose chases trying to find the right answers.

In this case, the Senator was attempting to manipulate Mark to make a point that is false. Didn't we already talk about manipulative people?

In order to improve the quality of your questions, you must have a proper technique. But before you can develop your technique, you must understand the types of questions available for your questioning toolkit.

In this section I'll talk about:

1) The types of questions available for your toolkit
2) How to embed the critical elements in your questioning technique
3) An effective questioning technique for internal auditors

4 TYPES OF QUESTIONS FOR YOUR TOOLKIT

There are multiple types of questions that can be used to effectively communicate with people. The two most basic are closed and open.

Closed Questions

Closed questions are either on or off, yes or no? For example, if I ask someone, "Did you submit the paperwork?" They can either answer yes or no.

Closed questions are good for:

- Getting specific information.
- Confirming facts.
- Making a decision.

Unfortunately, Senator Sullivan thought he was confirming a fact when he said to Zuckerberg "Only in America, right. You couldn't do this in China". He was sadly mistaken. Jack Ma, Ma Huateng, and William Ding are Chinese billionaires who own Alibaba, TenCent and NetEase worth $42 billion, $51 billion and $18 billion respectively.

Closed questions at the wrong time can kill a conversation. In the video, notice how Zuckerberg shut down when talking with the Senator. When you do this, your audit clients also shut down.

Earlier, we talked about the arrogant auditor. The arrogant auditor over uses closed questions because she is constantly trying to confirm what she already knows. Much like the Senator, what you think you know may be inaccurate.

If you want to get specific information, confirm facts, make a decision or test your understanding, closed questions are great for that. If you're asking Mark Zuckerberg about becoming a multi billionaire in America, not so much.

Open Questions

Open questions seek to understand others thoughts, ideas and feelings. As the name implies, they are very open. Answers are typically more than just a yes or no.

Open questions are good for getting broad information about a person, place or process. For auditors, open questions are really good for encouraging discussion. They often begin with what, why or how.

It's easy to ask closed questions, but open questions require a little more thought and work. Here's a little trick to help you create open questions.

You can turn closed questions into open questions by adding one of the following phrases to sentences:

- Tell me
- Can you describe
- Can you show me
- To what extent
- How do you feel about

Here's an example. Suppose you ask an audit client,

"Is this area well controlled?"

This is not a good question for getting to know an area. The response is either yes or no. Neither answer provides valuable information. However, if you want to spark conversation, you can turn this closed question into an open one by saying,

"Can you describe the controls for this area?"

What if you ask a client,

"Have you ever experienced fraud in the area?"

Again, another bad closed question that can be made better by adding one of our phrases. How does this sound?

"Can you tell me about the last fraud that occurred in this area?"

In this example, the client is forced to provide more than a yes or no answer. Open questions are great for understanding the processes in your organization.

Clarifying Questions

Clarifying questions are a close cousin to closed questions. They are simple questions of fact. They clarify a specific dilemma and don't provide any additional information. They are often confused with probing questions, but there is one big difference between probing and clarifying questions. The person being asked the question does not have to think before answering. The answer should be at their fingertips. This is not saying that they may not have to look the information up, but the person does not have to apply critical thinking techniques or assumptions to answer clarifying questions.

Suppose you are asking a client a question about a missing transaction and you say,

"When did you notice the amounts were incorrect?"

The client responds, "Saturday at 12pm."

You wanted to know when they noticed something strange. They gave a factual answer that did not require critical thinking. This is a clarifying question.

Probing Questions

Probing questions help gain greater insight into a situation. They help uncover the reasons and emotions behind situations. Essentially, they help you to get closer to the root cause of problems. Probing questions are a type of open question and are good for:

- Gaining clarity to ensure that you have the whole story and that you understand it.
- Drawing information out of people who may be avoiding telling you the whole story.
- Gathering information.

Used ineffectively, probing questions can give the wrong results. Auditors often believe they are using probing questions when they are actually using clarifying questions.

Let's take a look at 14 probing questions auditors can ask.

Suppose you're doing fieldwork and find that something has allegedly gone awry. You want to determine the truth. You can start with question 1.

Question 1

How do you know this is true?

Probing questions not only verify the truthfulness of a claim, they challenge assumptions and beliefs. This question forces clients to think about project results and conclusions.

Question 2

How did you come to this conclusion?

This seems like a fairly easy question. However, it requires the person to walk through their thought process and it gives insight to both auditor and client. This insight can be used to determine the root cause of problems and to recognize patterns that may not have otherwise been recognized

Question 3

What impact do you think this will have?

What you're looking for here is an opinion from your audit client. They are the expert on their processes and should be able to predict a positive or negative consequence from the audit observation. You are simply asking them to predict the impact. This is helpful in determining the impact to present in your final audit report.

Question 4

What is your prediction?

The prediction question can be extremely powerful. You're asking the person to use their thoughts and feelings combined with their knowledge to create a hypothesis of what they think might or did happen. This question can provide a good understanding of the situation, but should not be relied upon exclusively.

Question 5

What is your biggest fear regarding this situation?

Asking someone their fear or the worst case scenario can provide a great deal of insight. As an auditor, it can help you determine the significance of a potential issue. For the client, it can help put things into perspective. It may put clients on high alert or help them realize the issue was not as serious as they thought.

Question 6

Does the same problem exist elsewhere in the organization?

This question is important because it helps manage risk at multiple levels. As an auditor, you can extend your coverage beyond this individual department and address systemic issues. And who better to give you insight on those issues than the client?

Question 7

What do you think is the root cause of the problem?

Every problem has a root cause. Every client has insight into root causes. It is important that auditors leverage client's knowledge to solve problems.

Question 8

What was your intention?

This question is great because you get an understanding of a person's thought process. Intent can be different from delivery. And this question helps you determine what the original plan was, how it went awry, and what knocked it off track.

This question also gives insight into people's character. Many perpetrators of white collar crimes started out with good intentions.

Question 9

Do you feel this is right?

On one hand this question could be a test of the client's ethical decision making abilities. On the other hand, it could be a test of logical reasoning capabilities. Either way, this question allows clients to examine the conclusions they've reached.

Question 10

What do you think the solution is?

This is more of an upbeat question because you're asking them to tell you what they believe will solve the problem. Whether it's monetary resources, human resources, or just attitude issues, employees often know how to solve problems they face on the job.

But this is another one of those questions that can be taken multiple ways. One client might respond with a well thought out solution, whereas another may suggest firing the boss.

Question 11

What would your ideal outcome be?

This question is different from, "what do you think the solution is?" because a person's ideal outcome could be differ from the ultimate solution for the greater good.

Question 12

What would need to change in order for you to accomplish this?

This question is aimed at getting the client to think about the process and which changes would need to be made within it to achieve the goal.

Question 13

What are the pros and cons?

When facing difficult situations we oftentimes focus on one or the other, leading to a skewed answer. But getting clients to focus on both will give a more well rounded answer to the business question.

Question 14

Is this problem causing other problems?

This question aims to find if there is a ripple effect for the issue at hand.

Asking clients these 14 questions will help you probe a situation and find the answers you need to complete your audit engagements.

Summary

There are two basic types of questions, closed and open questions. Closed questions are very good for getting direct answers or confirming what we already know. Open questions are very good if you want a discussion or to stimulate some dialogue or get someone's opinion.

Both questions are useful to internal auditors. But you must develop an appropriate strategy to know when to use which type of question. Before I get to that, I'll next put the 5 Critical Elements for Quality

Questions into perspective. I discussed them earlier, but next I'll dig a little deeper.

5 CRITICAL ELEMENTS FOR QUALITY QUESTIONS

As mentioned, the 5 elements are important. The audience must be appropriate, the timing accurate, the tone good, the place adequate and the technique must fit the situation.

Finding your audience

Finding the right person to question is critical. Imagine how much time you can waste explaining things multiple times to different people. That is exactly what happens when you do not take time to ensure that you have the appropriate person

Here are four questions you can ask to find the appropriate person:

Who was responsible for this process?

Most likely, they'll tell you the primary person in charge. This is important, write that name down. But then ask

Who do they obtain information from?

Every process requires some sort of information and your client is getting information from someone else in order to make that process happen. You will probably need to talk to that person too.

After this, it is important to understand...

Who receives this information once it's complete?

The person performing the process may be getting information from someone, but once their part is complete, they must be providing some sort of information to someone else. It's important to understand where the information is coming from, how it is being processed and what happens when it is passed along to someone else.

Is there anyone else that's involved in this process?

Ah. Now that's a closed question. We can turn it into an open question by saying,

"Who else is involved in this process?"

There. That's a better question. It helps identify other people who may help you get a good understanding of the operations.

Your 4 good probing questions are:

- Who is responsible for the process?
- Where are they getting the information from?
- Who receives the information after they do their part?
- Is there anyone else involved in the process?

Once you start to ask this series of questions, you will be able to accurately identify and define your audience. Now that you know who to talk to, when can you talk to them.

Timing is everything.

The last thing you want to do is abuse your audit clients time. Timing should be relatively simple. You want to determine timing for the department and for the individuals within the department.

For department's, think about busy times of the day, week, month, quarter or year. To find the right time, all you have to do is ask.

What are your busy time periods?

For example, accounting departments are obviously busy at the end of the month or the end of the quarter. So you don't want to disturb an accounting department at these times.

You'll want to find out what times work best for the department.

You should also consider timing for the individual people within the department. You may have some people in departments that take certain times off during the year.

When I worked in higher education, it was customary to close campuses between Christmas and New Years. Oftentimes people began taking vacation sooner or they extend it afterward. As a result, you knew to be careful about the timing of audit interactions.

You want to find out what time of day is good for your audit clients. I worked with one senior vice president in an organization who would always called lunch meetings. He said he was most productive at lunch.

I know what you're thinking. Lunch time is your personal time. But it wasn't all bad because he would always provide lunch.

So after you've found your audience, determine a good time for them. And while you're interacting with clients, be nice to them.

Watch your tone when you're talking to people.
The tone you use can really be an indicator of your inner emotion.

Consider the following sentence.

I love auditors.

Three simple words. Now let's take a look at how tone can disclose the true meaning of a sentence.

Imagine someone saying,

I love auditors.

Stressing the first word. I. What does that convey?

What this tells me is the person making the statement likes auditors, however, others in the department don't feel the same way.

Try this one.

I *love* auditors.

Emphasis on the word *love* now makes that sentence sound somewhat sarcastic.

How about this one? What does this say to you?

I love *auditors*.

See now again That sounds like I just truly hate orders. That's not even sarcastic. The tone you use counts.

The Place is Important

Earlier I gave examples of people popping questions in inappropriate places. Remember the young man who asked Jill for her hand in marriage in a Starbucks. For her, that was not the appropriate place.

I remember wrapping up an audit and the client invited us to lunch. The place was full of busy business people rushing to get their daily dose of nutrients before heading back to the office to finish the day.

Service was slow. We began to have casual conversations about the organization. At some point, one of the audit team members began asking specific questions. The Vice President of the organization gave the auditor a menacing stare and politely said, "This is not the place to talk about this."

The place you chose to have discussions is important. Finding the proper place can propel your questions from being a necessary nuisance to an effective audit communication tool.

The proper place is like going out on a date. Or the place after the date. You know, the whole your place or mine? And much like preparing for a date, you want to make sure that your house is in order. There are so many things that can affect the ambiance of your location.

For example, you don't want clients, sitting in your conference room located on the corner where the sun shines directly in their eyes during afternoon meetings. Similarly, you don't want the sound of the jackhammer from the city street coming in and corrupting your conversations. And don't get me started on the temperature.

The place that you select to have conversations vastly affects the quality of your outcomes.

LET'S TALK TECHNIQUE

Now that you are familiar with the types of questions, when do you use them. You should be familiar with the 3 phases of an audit project: planning, fieldwork and reporting. For each phase, certain questions are more effective than others.

In the traditional model, the planning phase was conducive to open questions, the fieldwork phase to probing questions, and the reporting phase closed questions.

Suppose you are planning for an audit and meet with the client to discuss the area. A decent planning open question might be:

Tell me about your area.

The client then describes the processes, thus providing enough insight for you to plan the audit.

Suppose you find several issues during the fieldwork phase. You now begin asking probing questions,

What sort of impact do you think this will have?

What is your biggest fear about this?

What do you think is the root cause?

Then you enter the reporting phase. During the reporting phase you began to ask closed questions to confirm your factual observations.

You've told me that a million dollars is missing. Is this true?

Our test results found that there are no controls in place for this process. Are the results accurate?

The client will answer either yes or no. Then you begin writing an audit report.

This funnel technique has been a great time-tested model for asking questions while auditing, but I'm proposing a new model. One in which we flip this one on its head, literally and figuratively, so that we can ask better questions, get better answers and perform better audits.

Figure 3 - The Old Model for Asking Questions in the Audit Process

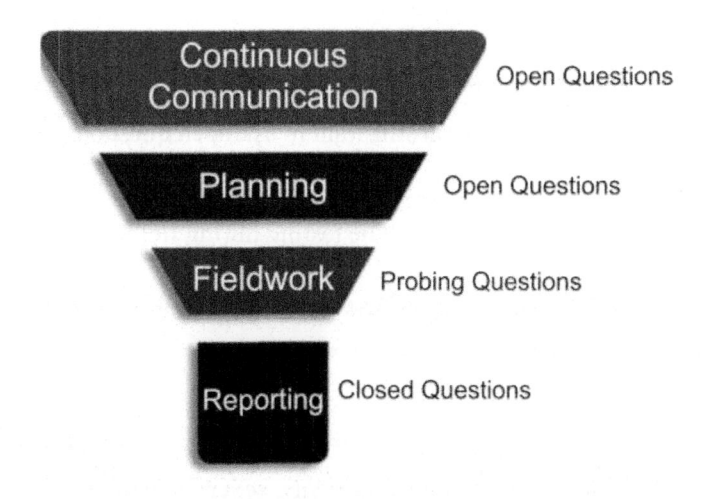

Continuous Communication — Open Questions
Planning — Open Questions
Fieldwork — Probing Questions
Reporting — Closed Questions

Recall the old model required you to ask open questions during audit planning, probing questions during fieldwork, and closed questions during the reporting phase.

What I'm proposing is something similar, but light years better. During our planning phase, you still want to ask open questions because that gets your client's talking about their area. That also helps you form the basis of what you will be testing during fieldwork.

What I am now proposing is that we break fieldwork up into two sections.

In the first fieldwork section, you're still going to ask probing questions, but you're also going to introduce several hypothetical questions. Hypothetical questions encourage clients to consider new ways of dealing with situations. It forces them to think through scenarios that could solve the problem. Questions 4, 10 and 12 in the probing questions list lean hypothetical. Hypothetical questions should be designed to help clients identify and explain the actual issues. Try something like:

-What could have caused this to happen?

-How do you think this occurred?

In other words, the hypothetical questions will help perform a root cause analysis. Answers obtained here will be the basis for the cause in your audit report. Then, you close out the first phase of fieldwork by asking closed questions to confirm the legitimacy of the issue(s).

Now that you've confirmed that there is an issue, it's time to move to the second fieldwork phase. Here you're going to ask hypothetical questions again, but this time the purpose is to get the client to discuss the potential impact of the issue. Your clients know how (or can speculate how) their processes can potentially impact their department, other departments, and possibly the entire organization. You simply need to ask. Try something like:

-How could this impact your area?

-How could this impact other areas?

Next, you're going to ask closed questions again. But this time you are confirming the potential impact. Honing your hypothetical questions help clients come up with the causes and cures of audit issues.

If you recall, in her book *Smart Questions: The Essential Strategy for Successful Managers*, Dorothy Leeds said, "The only way you help someone accept an idea as his own is to ask him a question and let him give the answer back to you." Allowing your clients to assist in discovering solutions yields better buy in to the final audit report. This is a win for everyone.

You are finally ready to produce your audit report. Most audit reports fall flat because you fail to present appropriate risks, impacts and recommendations. You've tried to use the Institute of Internal Auditor's 5c's, but have had mediocre success. If this sounds familiar, you're in luck. I have a solution that will help you develop better audit issues.

7 QUESTIONS FOR SUCCESSFUL AUDIT ISSUES

Every audit issue should clearly describe the problem, the impact, proposed solutions, and a commitment to reducing the risks. Answering the following questions will help you create meaningful audit report issues.

1. What is wrong?

Your audit report should clearly describe the problem. Ideally, the answer to this question should be the first sentence. It lets your clients know what is wrong without wading through unnecessary paragraphs.

2. Why is it wrong?

This question describes the criteria (policy, procedure, best practice, law, rule, etc) that was not followed. Suppose company policy requires bank reconciliations every 30 days, but the department prepares them every 60. You would describe the violation of policy here.

3. What is the impact?

You should have already obtained this answer during fieldwork while asking hypothetical questions. Include this information in the report so that your clients understand the significance of the issue.

4. How can it be fixed?

Similar to the impact, you should have obtained this answer while asking hypothetical questions during fieldwork. This is your audit issue recommendation.

5. Who can/should fix it?

You must assign an owner to every issue. Asking client's (or yourself) this question helps ensure you have the appropriate people assigned to fix the issue.

6. When can it be fixed?

Due dates are important. They help ensure management mitigates risks timely. This question helps determine the timing of fixing audit issues. But again, you should have already obtained this information during fieldwork.

7. Is there any additional context required?

Your audit issues should be clear and concise. Ask yourself if there is enough context for the audience to read each item and understand what it means to the organization. Each issue must be able to stand on its own. It is important to consider your audience. They range from line level workers to Board members. You must make sure there is sufficient context to clearly communicate the concern.

Incorporating these 7 questions into your overall technique will help you to ask better questions, get better answers, perform better audits and write better reports. Yes, the quality of your questions during fieldwork impacts the speed and quality within which you prepare your report.

Figure 4 - The New Model for Asking Questions in the Audit Process

Stage	Question Types
Continuous Communication	Open Questions
Planning	Open Questions
Fieldwork	Probing, Open, Clarifying, Hypothetical, Closed
Fieldwork	Probing, Open, Clarifying, Hypothetical, Closed
Reporting	7 Questions for Successful Audit Issues
Continuous Communication	Open Questions

STEP 4 - MAKE A COMMITMENT TO CLARITY

Instead of seeking clarity in conversations, humans have a habit of jumping to conclusions prematurely. This habit kills productivity and ruins relationships and interactions.

Recall my Las Vegas concert debacle. While on the phone with the venue worker I heard one thing while he was actually saying something else. I believed he communicated to me that tickets were still available and, if I arrived early enough, I could snag a seat to see one of my favorite old school hip hop artists. He thought that he was telling me to get there early to beat the crowd to pick up tickets that I had already purchased. Neither one of us was being deceptive. We simply had a misunderstanding. A misunderstanding that could have been avoided if we had committed to clarity in our conversations.

Recall the situation anticipation example in which Tammi jumped to conclusions about her boyfriend Joe. She thought he was about to ask for her hand in marriage, but he had another surprise for her. She ended up embarrassing herself. Not only that, she ruined her relationship with an otherwise good guy who had fallen on bad times. This happened because she didn't seek clarity in the conversation.

When talking to the venue worker about the concert, I should have asked a few clarifying questions. Before speaking to her boyfriend, Tammi should have done the same.

As an auditor, you don't ever want to leave an area without confirming the things that you've observed. You can do this by paraphrasing. After a client has disclosed something, follow up with some of the following 5 phrases that help paraphrase the conversation.

5 QUESTIONS THAT PROMOTE PARAPHRASING

1. You think that...

And then describe what it is that you think you've heard them say.

While on the phone with the concert worker, if I had simply said, "You think that I'll be able to buy tickets and get in if I arrive that early?", things would have been different.

This would have let him know that I believed tickets were still available. This would have saved me a lot of headache.

When talking to her boyfriend about the surprise gift, if Tammi had just said, "Do you think we're ready for marriage?" Joe could have explained what was happening.

Questions are typically better than statements.

2. So what you're saying is...

And then describe what you think the client said.

If I had simply asked the venue worker, "So what you're saying is tickets are still available?"

He would have immediately corrected me.

If that question doesn't suit your situation, you can try.

3. Did I hear you say...

And then describe what you believe you've heard.

While on the phone with the venue worker, if I had simply said, "Did I hear you say tickets are still available?", he would have quickly corrected me.

If you want to be more direct, you can use Question number four.

4. Is this what you said?

Repeat what you thought you heard. Then ask this question.

The other party should provide feedback quickly. This works especially well for auditors after reviewing a process. If you can explain it back to a client and they agree, you know you understand it.

5. Did I explain that correctly?

With this question, you explain your interpretation of the discussion.

If the client answers yes. Congratulations, you now understand the process. If no, begin asking clarifying questions.

Step 5 - The Communication Continuum

You've worked hard to build a collaborative environment. Don't let the only time your clients see you is when you're coming to audit. Let's make it a continuous communication environment. Here's how.

First, create a client log.

Now I know that might sound strange. But if you create a log, then you know who all of your clients are. Identifying them as the first step. You can not establish relationships with people you have not acknowledged exist.

When you create the log, you know who your clients are. There may be members on your staff who have relationships with audit clients that you might be that you might not be aware of.

For example, you might have a staff auditor who has a fairly decent relationship with a director or senior vice president at your organization.

It's time to play matchmaker.

Second, find the best fit and time

So what you want to do here is find the best fit, Now that you have a client log, find out who on your team is the best fit to have a relationship with each client.

In other words, pair clients with auditors from your department who best match the client's communication style. Just because you're in charge, that doesn't mean you should be the only one in charge of relationship-building activities.

Now, work the log. Visit clients and notate when they were contacted and by whom. You want to have some accountability for when you're seeing them because it helps you realize when you might be neglecting some clients.

So create the log to have awareness of who your clients are. You work the log so that you can ensure that you're visiting them on a regular basis.

Third, give a presentation.

I was flattered a few years ago when one of my clients asked me to do it for a presentation for their entire unit. The unit consisted of about 100 people. I did a fraud presentation. They asked us back the next year. I did it for about four years in a row. This was great exposure for our department. I'm told it humanized us. There are multiple ways that you can have continuous contact and continuous communication with your audit clients. Giving a presentation is a great relationship building tool.

Fourth, assist in Interviews
I've been asked to sit in on several interviews and quite frankly, it's been a really good experience because it shows that your clients value your opinion. Also, you get to meet candidates before they start working. On their first day, you already know who they are. This helps your relationship build a bunch.

Always try to create a continuous communication process with your audit clients.

Conclusion

Auditors and Business Consultants play an important role in helping organizations run efficiently. Asking what's wrong, dissecting issues and helping people discover solutions is an important part of what we do. To be effective at this, you must be able to ask good quality questions. I hope that you see the art of asking questions for auditors in a new light after reading this book. I want to see your career catapult. This is just the start. Go out there and Ask Better Questions, Get Better Answers and Perform Better Audits.

Printed in Great Britain
by Amazon